Nadiya's FAMILY FAVOURITES

Over 100 easy recipes for every kind of day

Photography by *Chris Terry*

MICHAEL JOSEPH *an imprint of* PENGUIN BOOKS

Contents

For the walls that shelter me from the wind.
To the roof that keeps the rain out.

You are my bricks and mortar:

Abdal, Musa, Dawud and *Maryam*

Food for all the family

Food is such a simple word. A simple four-lettered word that can evoke every human emotion possible. For me, food is all about the people we love, and the family memories we make with them, the things we eat as vivid in our minds as the moments and milestones that inspire them.

It's the look on my sister's candlelit, hand-over-mouth face as I walked into a darkened room with a sticky-sweet fondant-covered cake that took five days to make. While I worried it may be dry on the inside, nobody else cared, because it was spectacular on the outside and was met with the type of reaction every celebration cake should warrant: excitement, shock, maybe even a little Oscar-worthy acting, the kind where she knew she'd be getting a cake but pretended she wasn't expecting one, because that is what grown-ups do.

The sigh of satisfaction from my husband when I hand him a plate of wheat-crusted chicken at the end of a hard day clearing up the garage (a job he insists on doing on a weekly basis!). Showered, cleaned-up, lounge pants on, I sneak his dinner into our 'flounge' (the fun lounge), followed by Cookie Dough Ice Cream for afters, which always goes down a treat . . .'If you don't tell the kids, then I won't'. He eats, no words, just 'mmmms' and 'aaaahs', till he reaches his last morsels and says, 'I could do that all over again,' and yes, we are still on the subject of food. For him, every tiny plate of something delicious takes him to a wonderful place. He doesn't stay there long, but he knows he will be back again soon, since a mealtime is always around the corner.

The unsure face of my little man Moses (not so little any more!) back when he took his first mouthful of homemade Ginger Rice, as I came at him slowly with a neon plastic spoon and his eyes crossed till they could cross no more. That first taste of food as he wondered at the unfamiliar texture in his mouth. While we captured the moment in our minds, he pulled eagerly at my hand for more, his eyeballs playing tennis, from bowl to spoon and back again. Nothing has changed. He still eats everything cautiously, inspecting the texture and flavours, but almost always ending in a smile, to be met by my proud mummy face, and his curiosity satisfied.

My younger son, Mr David, declaring, 'Your cooking is yummy, Ma, but what's the point in eating when we could be playing video games and doodling?' The line 'think of all the poor people out there who have no food' never worked on him. His clear response: 'Well, we can give them my food then,' and the battle lost! He eats when it suits him, but it's a long slow process, and never as fast as his speedy comebacks. While he talks of everything but the food at our table, my mission is always to change his sceptical mind, success summed up by a hug from behind as he peers through the gap in my arms and mutters, 'Forget video games, that was much better.'

Then there's my bafflement at my almost gender-balancing pink in the family, Mary Moo, so sure of herself at just seven years old. She has a particular way with food: she enjoys eating everything, but is very specific; she loves a cashew, but always salted. 'I like taste,' she says. And never all at once. Like a bird, she picks all day: nuts, cheese, water, grapes, raisins. Literally the whole day her mouth can keep going, with strategically placed gaps to tell me where I am going wrong in life.

This is my family, and this book will give you a taste of the way we live our lives, with food for every kind of day. It's full of what we eat to keep us going through our weekly routine of every extracurricular activity known to man. These are the recipes that feed the five of us every day and a gang of many more for gatherings. For a family outing, we'll take our Samosa Pie and Chaat in a Bag for a picnic in the park. On manic weekdays, we're more likely to be cramming Not Prawn Toast in the back of the car before swimming lessons. If it's a wind-down weekend, you'll find us relaxing at home in our lounge pants and cooking Sunday Lunch Our Way, and when we've got people to stay, I serve up a spread so large that even the dining table will not suffice, and we have to deploy the countertops, for my Special Beef Curry and Chapattis to start with, then plenty else to follow! You'll find all the recipes I've mentioned and a lot more within these pages.

Food is not just the fuel that keeps us going, it isn't just a tick box, done! Food is one of the many things we take for granted, and because it's always been there, we assume it will never go away. Food has been my comfort many times. Somehow a cup of tea and a slice of Orange Coffee Poke Cake really do make life's troubles feel a little better, no matter how temporary the relief. Food gives us life, makes us smile, makes us weep, makes us feel emotions we did not think possible – and best of all, it helps us make memories.

Food is such a simple word. But those simple four letters underpin so much: my four walls, my roof, my radiators, my loves, my laughter. Food, home, family: for me, all three go hand in hand.

'Food is such a simple word. But those simple four letters underpin so much: my four walls, my roof, my radiators, my loves, my laughter.'

Breakfast

The last thought in my head every night before I go to bed is what we might have for breakfast in the morning. As I leave the kitchen I do a quick final scan of the grounds. Freezer: frozen fruit. Fruit bowl: over-ripe mango. Cupboards: toasted coconut. Fridge: sausages. Basket: eggs. Then I head upstairs with my mind full of recipes: could I make Fattoush, Bircher, Vermicelli, Crêpes, Shakshuka? I go to sleep happy in the knowledge that tomorrow I will win the breakfast game, because I know that whatever I make will be met with a triple, 'Thanks, Mum! Dad always just gives us cereal.' One-nil to me! Breakfast is perhaps the speediest meal in our house, mainly because it has to be. We break our fast fast, in between packing PE kits and locating lost socks. It happens even quicker if I say the word crêpes. (I'm even trying to write it quietly . . . shhh, they might hear!) But breakfast is also the meal that sets the troops up for a long day, so whatever we have, it must be delicious and filling, despite being rushed. They come home talking about their breakfast daydreams, and that, for me, makes it all worthwhile.

MAKES 12-14

PREP 15 MINS

COOK 30 MINS

INGREDIENTS

500g sweet potatoes
(about 2 medium
potatoes)

3 cloves of garlic

1 tsp salt

200ml whole milk

2 medium eggs

150g self-raising flour,
sifted

1 tsp baking powder

a large handful of fresh
dill, chopped, plus extra
for sprinkling

spray oil

vegetable oil, for frying

eggs, for frilly eggs

cracked black pepper,
for sprinkling

Most people don't own a waffle iron, and I avoid specialist equipment wherever I can. But that shouldn't stop us making waffles, so I've found another way! These are savoury with a touch of sweetness, beautifully orange from the mashed sweet potatoes, and laced with dill and a kick of garlic. It's such a lovely recipe for the weekend, and even better when the kids get involved. Stick a frilly egg on top and it's like heaven on a Saturday morning.

METHOD Put the sweet potatoes directly on the microwave plate. On the highest setting, cook them for 8 minutes. Once they are done they should be soft and the skin should cave in under the smallest pressure. Use oven gloves to take them out of the microwave, as they will be hot!

I would leave them for at least 15 minutes before you try to scoop out the flesh. Once they have cooled enough to handle, cut them in half lengthways and use a spoon to remove the flesh. Pop it into a blender. Add the garlic and salt and blend until you have a smooth purée.

Now add the milk, eggs, flour and baking powder, and blend again until you get a smooth paste.

Transfer the mixture to a jug. Add the chopped dill, mix well and set aside.

Place a griddle pan on a low to medium heat and spray it with oil. Spoon a ladleful of the mixture into each corner of the pan and fry for 6–7 minutes on one side, then turn over and cook for another 6–7 minutes on the other.

Place the waffles on a plate, covered with foil to keep them warm, and continue making them in this way until all the batter has been used. They freeze really well, so if you make more than you need, pop the extra ones into a freezer bag and reheat them in the oven from frozen when you need them.

I like to serve these waffles topped with a frilly fried egg, with a runny yolk. For the best frilly eggs, pop a small non-stick frying pan on to a high heat and add about 4 tablespoons of vegetable oil per egg. When the oil is smoking, add the egg. It should instantly frill round the edges if the oil is hot enough. Using a spoon, scoop some of the hot oil from under the egg and pour it over the white. This will help to cook the whites and avoid any uncooked, slimy bits, which are just not OK to eat!

Serve the waffles topped with the fried eggs and with a little extra dill and cracked black pepper sprinkled over.

MAKES 12

PREP 25 MINS

COOK 30 MINS

Crêpes are serious business in our house. I need only say the word and everyone goes into overdrive till they get a crêpe (or 12) into their belly. I once tried to pass off shop-bought ones as my own, but my kids looked at me like I came down with last night's shower. No fooling those crêpe connoisseurs. This is my variation on traditional crêpes, made sweeter by the addition of blitzed dates. They're great topped with cool yoghurt and this warm apple and walnut compote. Step away from the chocolate spread!

INGREDIENTS

For the crêpes

100g pitted dates (weight after pitting)

150ml boiling water

50g molasses

20g unsalted butter, melted

425ml whole milk

1 medium egg

150g self-raising flour, sifted

½ tsp baking powder

a large pinch of salt

spray oil

Greek yoghurt, to serve

For the compote

3 small green apples, peeled, cored and chopped

2 tbsp unsalted butter

30g soft dark brown sugar

½ tsp grated nutmeg

juice and zest of ½ a lemon

50g walnuts, roughly chopped

METHOD Put the dates in a bowl with the hot water and leave to plump up for 20 minutes, or at least until the water has cooled to room temperature.

In a blender, whiz the water and dates to a smooth paste. Add the molasses, butter, milk, egg, flour, baking powder and salt, and blitz until it is again a smooth paste. Transfer to a jug. If you're making the batter the night before, cover it with clingfilm and leave in the fridge until morning.

Put a medium non-stick saucepan on a medium to high heat. Add the apples, butter, sugar, nutmeg and lemon, and cook for 5–7 minutes until the apples are starting to soften and are just breaking down at the edges. Take off the heat and stir in the chopped walnuts.

Pop a pancake pan or a small non-stick frying pan (I use a 20cm pancake pan) on to the hob on a high heat. Spray with just a very light coating of oil.

When making crêpes, the first few are usually test ones, to determine if the batter is too loose or too thick. A little treat for the cook!

Spoon about 3 tablespoons of batter into the centre of the pan, then swirl it around till the entire pan base is covered in a thin layer of batter. If it moves too slowly and you are struggling to cover the base, add a little more milk to the mixture, stir well to loosen, and try making another pancake. If the batter is too loose and you find it is too translucent in the pan, add a tablespoon of flour and mix in well. Now make another crêpe.

Fry the crêpes for 2 minutes, or until the top surface looks matt. Flip over, using a palette knife or spatula, and cook for another minute. Lay the crêpe flat on a plate, then keep making more and popping them on top of one another. Keep the pile covered with foil, so they stay warm. You may find the hob needs adjusting between high and medium as you go along. The crêpes will tell you if they need less or more heat.

I like to serve a couple of crêpes folded into triangles, with a large dollop of yoghurt and the apple and walnut compote right on top.

DATE CRÊPES
with Apple and Walnut Compote

I love food that can divide opinion or convince doubting minds, and the now-fashionable partnership of salty and sweet often does exactly that. It's my all-time favourite combination: not sickly but just sweet enough, with saltiness to balance it out. Maple bacon might sound unusual, but it must be tried. I've paired it with homemade peanut butter and popped them on crumpets. On this occasion, I'm not suggesting you make the crumpets. Let's face it, a crumpet kind of day is probably also a day when you need instant satisfaction, which usually comes directly out of a packet.

SERVES 3
MAKES 6 CRUMPETS

PREP 15 MINS

COOK 15 MINS

INGREDIENTS

For the maple bacon
2 tbsp unsalted butter

12 halal turkey rashers
(I like to use the halal
alternative, but you can
use streaky bacon)

2 tbsp maple syrup

*For the peanut butter
(makes 200g)*
200g salted peanuts

3 tbsp olive oil (you may
need a little more)

6 crumpets

METHOD Start by putting a large non-stick frying pan on a high heat. Drop in the butter, and as soon as it has melted, cut each rasher in half and add to the pan. (This just makes the eating part a little more attractive.) Cook on a high heat for about 3–4 minutes, until crisp, then turn over and cook for another 3–4 minutes.

Lower the heat to medium and add the maple syrup. Give the rashers a good stir, using a pair of tongs, and leave the syrup to thicken and coat the rashers. Turn the heat as low as it will go.

Now get started on the peanut butter. Put the peanuts and olive oil into a food processor and blitz until you get a smooth paste. It's up to you at this point whether to go for crunchy or smooth. If you like it crunchy, just stop blitzing as soon as you are happy with the consistency. But if, like me, you like it smooth, keep blitzing until you have a smooth paste that moves easily in the processor. If you find it isn't moving at all, just add one small spoon of oil at a time until it starts to move. First time I made peanut butter, I poured in too much, and let's just say that batch of peanut butter didn't make it into our bellies.

Keep an eye on the rashers and move them around if you need to. You will know they're ready when the maple syrup has glazed the rashers and isn't sitting in the bottom of the pan. Now turn off the heat.

Toast the crumpets to your liking. I like them crunchy on the outside and just soft in the middle. Smother them with the peanut butter and top each one with 4 bits of maple bacon. I want to tell you to enjoy your crumpets straight away – that's as it should be. But I had to save these for my boy and he enjoyed them stone cold. He was probably just very hungry.

HOMEMADE PEANUT BUTTER
AND MAPLE BACON on Crumpets

I once had a terrible bagel experience. I know it's a first-world problem, but humour me. Having popped into a cafe for breakfast, I ordered a toasted bagel with butter and jam. Simple, you'd think. There I waited with my cup of builder's tea until my bagel arrived, just the way I like it, slightly overdone – but with no sign of butter or jam. I enquired politely after my toppings and was informed they had none! As I sat there dipping a dry bagel into tepid tea, I found myself dreaming about what I wished I was eating, and my ultimate bagel recipe was born. Here it is, filled with salty mature Cheddar and sweet citrus marmalade, then lightly toasted. Bagels are chewy and charming in their own unique way. They don't need much, but a little goes a long way.

SERVES **4-5**

PREP **10 MINS**

COOK **20 MINS**

INGREDIENTS

4 bagels, sliced in half horizontally (or buy pre-cut ones, as I do)

4 heaped tbsp finely shredded marmalade (about 125g)

freshly ground black pepper

160g mature Cheddar cheese, sliced thinly

4 heaped tbsp full-fat mayonnaise

spray oil

METHOD Open up your bagels and smother the bottom half of each bagel with the marmalade. Be generous. Sprinkle kindly with black pepper on top of the marmalade. I like to be quite heavy-handed, so I do a three-finger pinch rather than a dainty two-finger one.

Place slices of cheese on top of the marmalade and pepper. Now sandwich together with the top halves of the bagels. Give them all a light press so that everything is securely in place.

Using a knife, smother the top of each bagel with mayonnaise. Make sure you have enough left to do the other side.

Spray a frying pan lightly with oil so you get a light mist of oil in the pan. Place 2 bagels mayo-side down in the pan (or all 4 if you have a pan large enough) and cook for 4–5 minutes. As they are cooking, use the back of a spatula to press each bagel down, this will encourage the whole lot to fuse.

Smother the other side of each bagel with mayonnaise and flip over. Cook for another 3–4 minutes. If the bagels are catching, just turn the heat down. They are ready when the bagels are fused with oozy melted cheese and the marmalade is hot and sticky.

Take them out. Give the pan a quick clean with kitchen paper, put it back on the heat, spray with oil and cook the other 2 bagels the same way (unless you have done all 4 at once).

Enjoy while they are still warm, and be vigilant with that hot marmalade. I must say I'm not good at listening to my own advice. Excuse me while I get some ice for my burnt tongue. Enjoy!

Growing up in a Bangladeshi home, we had rice every which way. My mum would even cook up rice for breakfast if we had too much left over from the night before. We'd line our stomachs with rice in the morning, in preparation for the rice at lunch, and let's not forget rice with dinner! It sounds like overload, but it was the staple in our home and we knew no different. Of course, these days there is less rice involved in my weekly cooking, as I like to vary things, but I do love making this fried rice recipe for my family, all wrapped up in an egg omelette. Best of all, you don't need leftovers for this recipe – you can make it simply because you want it!

SERVES 4

PREP 15 MINS

COOK 25 MINS

INGREDIENTS
For the fried rice
1 tbsp unsalted butter

1 small red onion,
finely chopped

1 tsp salt

½ a red pepper,
finely chopped

1 tomato, chopped

1 x 198g tin of
sweetcorn, drained

1 tsp chilli flakes

1 tsp coriander seeds,
lightly crushed

1 tsp onion seeds

125g cooked rice

25g fresh coriander,
roughly chopped

For the omelette
6 large eggs

50ml whole milk

1 tsp onion seeds
(nigella seeds)

a pinch of salt

spray oil

METHOD Put a medium non-stick pan on a high heat. Add the butter and as soon as it has melted, add the onion and salt. Cook for a few minutes till the onion has softened.

Add the red pepper, tomato and sweetcorn and cook until any extra moisture at the bottom of the pan has reduced – this should only take a few minutes.

Stir in the chilli flakes and coriander seeds, cook the spices for a minute, then add the rice. I like to use the ready-cooked rice in pouches for recipes like this. It's tedious trying to cook a tiny amount of rice, and the shop-bought gear will do just as well. Can you imagine my mother's horror? I can hear her voice: 'What do you mean, no leftover rice?' Stir the rice through until everything is well combined.

Transfer the rice mixture into a bowl and add the chopped coriander. By not adding the herbs during the cooking process, they keep their freshness – fresh fragrant coriander is better than cooked unidentifiable coriander!

Whisk the eggs, milk, onion seeds and salt together in a bowl.

Wipe the pan with some kitchen paper and put it back on the heat. Spray lightly with some oil. Add a quarter of the egg mixture to the hot pan, then lift and swirl the pan so the egg covers the base. Cook the egg for 2–3 minutes, until the surface is matt and there are no runny eggy bits. Add a quarter of the rice mixture to one half of the omelette and flip the other half of the egg over it.

Serve while still warm, and make the other 3 omelettes the same way.

CHEESE ROLLS with Curried Beans

With three children in the house, I always have a stash of cheese sticks in the fridge drawer, and I am not ashamed to admit that I love stringy cheese! Even so, I thought I'd find a way to make this not-very-adult cheese into something a bit more grown-up. So for this recipe I have encased the sticks inside buttery garlic bread and baked them until the cheese is molten and stringy. To go alongside, I've created a simple curried take on baked beans.

MAKES 12

PREP 20 MINS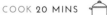

COOK 20 MINS

INGREDIENTS

For the cheese rolls

12 slices of white bread

12 stringy cheese sticks, unwrapped

1 egg, beaten

140g garlic butter, melted (if you can't find pre-made, just combine 140g melted salted butter with 4 crushed garlic cloves)

2 tsp paprika

For the curried beans

2 tbsp unsalted butter

2 cloves of garlic, crushed

2 small red onions, finely chopped

1 tsp salt

2 small green chillies, finely chopped (deseeded if you like less heat, or add more if you like extra heat)

2 tsp cumin seeds

2 tsp curry powder

2 x 415g tins of baked beans

a handful of fresh coriander, finely chopped

2 tbsp brown sauce

METHOD For the cheese rolls, preheat the oven to 200°C/180°C fan/ gas mark 6. Have a baking tray or two at the ready.

Using a rolling pin, roll out each slice of bread as flat as you can get it – this is quite a lot of fun, mainly because who knew bread could look like that?

Place a piece of cheese diagonally on a slice of bread. Roll the bread over the top and keep rolling until you have encased the cheese. Brush the edge with a little egg. Too much and it will make it slippery, so use just a little, and press the ends to seal.

Do the same to the rest of the slices and place them on the baking trays.

Stir the paprika into the garlic butter and brush it all over the rolls, not forgetting the underside. If any of them come apart or start to unravel, just give them a little squeeze.

Bake in the oven for 20 minutes. There may be some cheese escapees, but those are the crispy delightful bits.

While the rolls are baking, put a small non-stick pan on the hob on a medium heat. Add the butter and as soon as it has melted, add the garlic and cook for a minute or two. Add the onions and salt and cook until the onions have softened. This should take about 10 minutes.

Add the chilli, cumin seeds and curry powder and cook for about a minute, then add the beans and warm them through. Take off the heat and stir in the coriander and brown sauce.

Once the rolls are out of the oven, give them another brush with any leftover garlic butter from the baking tray and serve warm, with the curried beans.

CHAI SPICED VERMICELLI

When I was growing up, we used to eat this traditional recipe mostly at the weekends, but it has now become a regular weekday breakfast in my home, as an alternative to porridge. I have kept all the deliciousness of the whole spices used in the traditional recipe, but have replaced the butter and milk with coconut oil and coconut cream, making it a perfect breakfast for my vegan friends out there. It is warm, delicious and toasty, in all senses, and a perfect way to start the day. The aroma that will fill your kitchen and seep into your rooms is enough to rouse even the late wakers.

SERVES 4

PREP 10 MINS

COOK 25 MINS

INGREDIENTS

15g coconut shavings (or desiccated coconut)

100g wheat pasta vermicelli

1 cinnamon stick

1 bay leaf

1 cardamom pod

2 tbsp coconut oil

500ml coconut cream

40g caster sugar

METHOD Place a medium non-stick saucepan on the hob on a medium heat. Drop in the coconut and stir occasionally as it toasts. This should only take a few minutes, so do not leave the pan because it can burn quickly, as I've been reminded by my smoke alarm on several occasions.

Once the coconut is toasted, pop it into a bowl and set aside. Using dry kitchen paper, wipe out the pan to remove any stray bits of coconut.

Put the pan back on a medium heat and add the vermicelli. If yours is the kind that comes entwined like a bird's nest, gently crush it in your palms and drop it into the pan. This is quite a lot of fun, and I love the crunchy sound. If you have the pre-cut stuff, you will have a little less fun.

Toast the vermicelli until the strands are golden. Make sure to keep stirring and moving the noodles around – they toast unevenly, which makes them a beautiful patchy brown colour. If you need to walk away for a minute or so while you are toasting, just take the pan off the heat. Toasting should take around 5 minutes.

As soon as the noodles are ready, add the cinnamon stick, bay leaf and cardamom pod and toast for another 2 minutes. You will know it is ready when your nostrils are filled with the aroma of these beautiful whole spices.

Now add the coconut oil. If your oil is still in solid form, just stir it around until it has melted and has coated the vermicelli.

Stir in the coconut cream, then add the sugar and cook gently on a low heat to allow the spices to infuse and the mixture to thicken – this takes about 10 minutes. Don't cover the pan or it may boil over. It is ready when the bubbles slow down and the mixture has thickened and reduced.

Serve while it's hot, sprinkled with the toasted coconut you made earlier.

SERVES 8

PREP 20 MINS

COOK 10 MINS

Fattoush is a Middle Eastern salad, well known for the crisp, toasted bread bits that adorn the top. The mixture of different textures is what makes this one of my favourite salads to prepare and eat. But, as you may know by now, I cannot for the life of me leave any recipe alone! So this is my breakfast version, full of fresh, frozen and dried fruits and seeds, which means loads of variety. Not forgetting the most important part, the crispy bits on top, for which I've used toasted cinnamon tortillas.

INGREDIENTS

For the crispy tortillas

4 small flour tortilla wraps, cut into 1cm pieces

20g unsalted butter, melted

35g brown sugar

½ tsp ground cinnamon

a pinch of salt

For the fruit salad

400g fresh strawberries, hulled and quartered

1 large orange, peeled and segmented

125g dried pineapple, roughly chopped (I use scissors, much easier than a knife)

200g green grapes, halved

200g frozen blueberries

150g frozen raspberries

3 passion fruit, halved and pulp spooned out

2 tbsp sunflower seeds

25g fresh flat-leaf parsley, roughly chopped

METHOD Begin by making the crispy bits. Preheat the oven to 200°C/ 180°C fan/gas mark 6. Place the tortilla pieces on a large baking tray, so they can all sit in a single layer. Pour over the melted butter, then, using your hands, toss the tortillas around so each piece is coated. Sprinkle over the sugar and cinnamon and get in there, making sure everything is coated well. Sprinkle over the salt.

Pop into the oven and bake for 10 minutes, making sure to keep a close eye on the tortillas so they don't burn. Halfway through, take the tray out and turn the pieces around, then put back into the oven for another 5 minutes. You will know they are ready when they make a crunchy sound when dropped on to the tray. If you think they need a little longer, leave them for an extra few minutes, but make sure you still keep an eye on them.

Once they are crisp, leave them on the tray to cool and dry out a little bit more while you put the salad together.

Put all the salad ingredients into a large bowl and mix together. I like to do this just before serving, so that the frozen fruit stays frozen.

Serve in individual bowls and sprinkle those oh-so-delicious crispy bits over the top.

FRUIT SALAD FATTOUSH

SERVES 4

PREP 20 MINS

COOK 1 HOUR
55 MINUTES

INGREDIENTS

500g potatoes

3 tbsp olive oil

1 tbsp unsalted butter,
plus extra for greasing

1 white onion,
thinly sliced

1 tsp salt

1 tsp freshly ground
black pepper

6 sausages (I like to use
chicken, but you can use
whatever you prefer)

2 tomatoes, quartered
(about 230g)

2 tbsp ketchup

2 tbsp brown sauce

170g button mushrooms,
halved

1 x 200g tin of
baked beans

200ml chicken stock

4 eggs, for poaching

spinach, to serve
(optional)

I'm still a little bit afraid of fancy French words, but as I have learnt, most things can be translated. When they can be translated into a recipe, well then, it's a win-win! Boulangère is a method of cooking thin slices of potato in hot stock in the oven. It's my life's mission to cook potatoes in every which way and this is one of my favourites. This version includes the oven-cooking, and of course the potatoes, but with the extra love of a full English breakfast!

METHOD Preheat the oven to 200°C/180°C fan/gas mark 6. Lightly grease the base and sides of a 23cm square roasting dish or another similar-sized dish.

Peel and thinly slice your potatoes and leave them soaking in a bowl of water to prevent them browning.

Put a large non-stick frying pan on the hob on a medium to high heat. Add the oil and butter and as soon as the butter has melted, add the sliced onion along with the salt and pepper. Cook until the onion has softened. This should take about 5 minutes.

Using scissors, cut each sausage into 4 equal pieces. Add the sausages to the pan and fry them until they are cooked through. This should take about 10 minutes.

Add the tomatoes, ketchup, brown sauce and mushrooms and fry for 10 minutes, or until the mushrooms have cooked through and the tomatoes have broken down.

Take off the heat. Add the baked beans and stir in.

Drain the potatoes and pat dry, just to remove any excess moisture. Add the potatoes to the frying pan and mix until they are coated with everything else in the pan.

Throw everything into the prepared dish and push it all down a little. If there are stray potato slices, just straighten them out. Pour in the hot stock and bake for 1 hour, covering the dish with foil after 30 minutes.

It is ready when the potatoes can be pierced with a knife with no sign of resistance – if the knife glides straight through, the potatoes are done. Take the dish out of the oven and leave uncovered for 10 minutes before serving. It will be piping hot. These 10 minutes will give you just enough time to poach some eggs and wilt a little spinach too, to serve alongside it.

BREAKFAST BOULANGÈRE

SERVES 4

PREP 20 MINS,
PLUS OVERNIGHT
SOAKING

COOK 5 MINS

I discovered Bircher muesli only very recently, but now I've started seeing it pop up everywhere, in all my regular coffee hangouts. Meanwhile, something I'm no stranger to is lassi, a common drink at Indian weddings and in Indian restaurants. Lassi isn't normally my favourite drink in the world as I'm not a massive fan of how thick it is – I'm never sure whether to swallow, chew or neither! So I thought why not combine it with Bircher, to help my mouth make sense of it. With the loveliness of mango, mint and lime, all soaked into gorgeous oats, there is no longer any confusion: all you need is a spoon and an appetite.

INGREDIENTS

For the Bircher

100g flaked almonds

450g tinned mango pulp (you can find this in the world food aisles of most supermarkets and in Asian shops – or you could make your own, using fresh mango)

6 large fresh mint leaves, finely chopped

1 lime, juice and zest

200ml unsweetened almond milk

150g rolled porridge oats (not the jumbo ones)

For the topping

1 fresh mango (or a 420g tin of mango in syrup, drained), chopped into small pieces

a small handful of fresh mint, finely chopped

METHOD Toast the flaked almonds in a small non-stick frying pan on a medium to high heat. Toss them around till they are golden all over, then set aside in a bowl and leave to cool.

Put the mango pulp, mint, lime juice and zest into a large bowl (word of warning: make sure it's a bowl that fits into the fridge – I'm saving you some washing-up here). Pour in the almond milk and add half the toasted almonds. Stir well until everything is combined.

Add the oats and mix it all well, making sure the oats are completely covered in the fruity mixture. Cover with clingfilm and pop into the fridge overnight, ready for breakfast in the morning.

Next morning, take the bowl out of the fridge – the oats will have doubled in volume, as they will have soaked up a lot of the lassi liquid.

Make the topping by mixing the chopped mango and mint together. Serve in small bowls or jam jars, top with the mango, and sprinkle with the rest of the toasted flaked almonds. Surely a breakfast worth waiting all night for!

MAKES **9 SWIRLS**

PREP **30 MINS**

COOK **35 MINS**

It's almost as easy to make these as it is to buy them from that well-known Swedish furniture store that drains the life from your feet! Very like cinnamon swirls, but with coffee and chocolate instead, mine are topped with a sticky espresso icing. I'm a tea drinker – I have tried to drink coffee, but it never ends well. Put coffee in a sweet pastry, however, and I'm good to go!

INGREDIENTS

For the filling

1 tbsp unsalted butter, melted

2 tsp cocoa powder

2 tsp instant espresso powder (or coffee granules)

65g soft light brown sugar

100g dark chocolate, finely chopped (or chocolate chips)

For the dough

450g self-raising flour, plus extra for dusting

¼ tsp salt

2 tbsp caster sugar

100g unsalted butter, melted, plus extra for greasing

1 tsp vanilla bean paste

2 medium egg yolks

200ml whole milk, plus extra for glazing

For the icing

2 tbsp boiling water

2 tsp instant espresso powder (or coffee granules)

1 tbsp unsalted butter, softened

2 tbsp full-fat cream cheese

125g icing sugar, sifted

METHOD Make the filling first by mixing together the melted butter, cocoa, espresso powder, brown sugar and chocolate.

Grease a 20cm round loose-bottomed cake tin. Preheat the oven to 180°C/160°C fan/gas mark 4.

Put the self-raising flour, salt and sugar into a bowl and give it a quick mix. Put the melted butter, vanilla paste, egg yolks and milk into a smaller bowl, and whisk until combined.

Make a well in the centre of the dry ingredients and pour in the wet ingredients. Use a palette knife to mix it all in, then get your hands in and bring everything together until you have a smooth dough.

Throw a little flour on a work surface and roll out the dough to a rectangle about 30 x 25cm. Spread the filling evenly all over the dough, right to the edges. Then roll the dough up, starting from the long edge of the rectangle.

Cut the roll into 9 equal pieces and turn them on to their sides so you can see those beautiful swirls. Using the chubby part of your hands, give each a little push – this will encourage the rolls to stick together and reduce gaps. Place them on their sides in the prepared tin, making sure those swirls are on show. Brush with milk and bake for 30–35 minutes. They are ready when golden on top and the rolls are coming away from one another.

Leave to cool completely in the tin. This will help the icing to set better on top and not simply run off. You can eat these warm, but be warned, you will chase the icing, (which is not an awful thing, I suppose).

Make the icing by mixing together the boiling water and espresso powder. Give the mixture a few minutes to cool, then add the butter, cream cheese and icing sugar and mix until you have a thick coffee-flavoured icing. Drizzle the icing all over the top of the cooled swirls.

Take the swirls out of the tin and they are ready to serve. Now it's a case of identifying the biggest one and trying to tear it out of the bundle as politely as possible!

Mocha swirls

chocolate, *espresso coffee*, vanilla,

soft pastry, *Sticky icing*

SERVES 8

PREP 20 MINS

COOK 40 MINS

INGREDIENTS

200g semolina

3 cardamom pods

2 bay leaves

1 cinnamon stick

150g clarified butter (sometimes labelled as ghee)

600g raisins

120g soft light brown sugar

1 orange, zest only

500ml boiling water

1 x 500g block of puff pastry

plain flour, for dusting the surface

30g pistachios, roughly chopped

My mum used to make halva on special occasions, usually when we were celebrating something, like good exam results, successful driving tests or a pregnancy in the family. She'd find any excuse to make this sweet warm treat of toasted semolina, clarified butter, sugar, dried fruit and nuts. Traditionally it is eaten with a paratha, which is a buttery, flaky chappati, but to save time I have devised a recipe for a cheat's version. We always eat this with our hands, but there are many creative ways of eating it, and everyone works out their own favourite.

METHOD Place a large non-stick saucepan on a medium heat. Throw the semolina into the pan, then stir and dry-roast it until it is a light golden brown. This can take about 15 minutes, but be patient, it's worth it. Keep stirring and moving the semolina so the bottom doesn't catch.

Once the semolina is toasted, add the cardamom pods, bay leaves and cinnamon stick and warm through until the mixture is fragrant.

Add the clarified butter and mix until the butter has melted and the mixture is the texture of very wet sand. Add the raisins, brown sugar and orange zest and mix really well.

Now add the boiling water and stand back, as the mixture will bubble up. Be ready to stir. Keep stirring, and don't be tempted to stop, as this will prevent lumps. The mixture should be like a firm dough. Put a lid on the pan to keep the halva warm while you make the paratha.

Place a non-stick frying pan on a medium heat. Cut the puff pastry into 12 equal pieces. Dust a work surface, then take each piece of dough and roll it into a ball. All the rules of pastry-making can go out of the window. Don't worry about the lamination here.

Flatten each ball into a circle and roll out to a thickness of 3mm.

Place one pastry at a time in the hot pan and cook for 4 minutes, then turn over and cook for another 2 minutes. Once cooked, place the paratha on a plate and cover with foil to keep warm while you make the others.

Serve the parathas with the halva, topped with the chopped pistachios.

SEMOLINA HALVA
with Cheat's Paratha

I love a warm breakfast such as porridge when I'm enjoying a long, lazy, drawn-out morning. But sometimes, just sometimes, I fancy something a little bit different. So this is my alternative version made with ground rice. It's a long, slow cook but is worth the effort, especially the process of toasting the rice flour, which really enhances the overall flavour. Spiced with fragrant cardamom and topped with a tangy jam, it's porridge rethought and reinvented. It also happens to be gluten free.

SERVES 4

PREP 15 MINS

COOK 30 MINS

INGREDIENTS

For the porridge
140g ground rice
(or rice flour – they are
the same thing, but the
flour is finer)

2 cardamom pods,
seeds only

30g coconut oil

750ml rice milk

40g caster sugar

a pinch of salt

chopped pistachios, to
serve (optional)

For the raspberry rose jam
220g seedless
raspberry jam

5 organic roses, petals
removed (approx. 20g)
and finely sliced

3 drops of rose extract

METHOD For the porridge, place a medium non-stick pan on a medium heat. Add the rice flour to the pan. (Take off any extra layers of clothing because it can get warm.) Mix the flour around the pan – toasting it gives it an intense flavour. You need to toast it for about 15 minutes, until the flour is golden brown all over.

As soon as the flour is ready, add the cardamom seeds and mix through.

Add the coconut oil and stir until melted. The mixture should resemble wet sand.

Pour in the rice milk – this is the best bit, but stand back, as it will bubble up. Keep stirring till the mixture begins to thicken – this should take about 10 minutes.

Add the sugar and salt and continue to stir until the mixture has thickened to the consistency of porridge. Take off the heat and set aside to cool a bit.

Meanwhile, put the jam into a smaller non-stick pan and place on a medium heat. As soon as the jam warms up, stir in the rose petals and the rose extract. Heat until the petals have softened.

Serve the rice porridge with large dollops of the warm jam and sprinkled with chopped pistachios.

RICE PORRIDGE
with Raspberry Rose Jam

Sometimes I crave something really green to start the day, and this recipe is a great way to get loads of iron-rich spinach into the system first thing in the morning. It beats a bright green juice or smoothie concoction – I'd need the intentions of an angel to drink one of those. I will instead stick to my spinach shakshuka, which is cooked in a rich tomato sauce and finished with runny eggs on top. It's delicious served with yoghurt and toast.

SERVES 4

PREP 15 MINS

COOK 30 MINS

INGREDIENTS

3 tbsp olive oil

2 cloves of garlic, crushed

2 spring onions, finely chopped

½ tsp salt

1 tbsp tomato purée

4 tomatoes, chopped

2 tsp cumin seeds

1 tsp smoked paprika

200g baby spinach leaves

4 medium eggs

1 tsp chilli flakes

To serve

Greek yoghurt

toasted sourdough

METHOD Place a large non-stick frying pan (preferably one with a lid) on a high heat. Add the oil, and as soon as it is warm, add the garlic. Turn the heat down and add the spring onions.

Add the salt, tomato purée and chopped tomatoes and cook for about 5 minutes, until the tomatoes have softened, adding 2 tablespoons of water if they start catching on the bottom of the pan.

Add the cumin seeds and smoked paprika and cook the spices through for a few minutes.

Add the spinach, a handful at a time, and mix as best as you can – I know spinach can go rogue! Put the lid on the pan and allow the spinach to wilt. This will only take a few minutes.

Take off the lid and cook for another few minutes on a medium heat until all the moisture has dried up.

Make 4 cavities in which to place the eggs. Crack an egg into each cavity, then put the lid on top and leave on the heat until the whites are cooked and the yolks are still runny. This will take roughly 4 minutes. Take off the lid and sprinkle over the chilli flakes.

Spoon an egg and some of that smoky spinach on to each plate, and serve with yoghurt and crisp toasted sourdough.

SMOKY SPINACH SHAKSHUKA

Whenever we have guests over for the weekend, I like to make something really super-special for breakfast. I couldn't bear the idea of presenting a visitor with cereal, so I like to make something simple but really delicious and pleasing to the eye. That, for me, means three essential things: pastry, ham and cheese. What could be better? This crown is big enough to have for breakfast and still leave enough for a snack later on.

MAKES 10-12 SLICES

PREP 25 MINS

COOK 30 MINS

INGREDIENTS

2 x 320g packets of ready-rolled puff pastry

4 tbsp tomato ketchup

1 tsp paprika

12 cooked smoked turkey or ham slices

200g Gouda cheese, grated

1 egg, lightly beaten

rock salt

1 tsp black sesame seeds

METHOD Preheat the oven to 200°C/180°C fan/gas mark 6. Line a large baking tray with baking paper.

Unroll both pieces of pastry and join two of the short ends to make one long piece, pressing the two edges together. Place your long piece of pastry on a work surface, making sure to keep the pastry on the pieces of paper it comes wrapped in, as this will make manoeuvring much easier later on.

Mix the ketchup and paprika together in a small bowl and spread all over one side of the pastry, leaving just 1cm free round the edges. Lay the slices of turkey or ham on top, followed by the cheese.

Roll up the pastry like a Swiss roll, starting from the long edge. Try to roll it as tightly as possible. Once it's rolled, bring the two ends together to create a ring and join by squashing the pastry together.

Place the pastry ring on the prepared baking tray.

Using a sharp knife, cut 2cm-width slits around the edges, making sure not to go all the way through. Gently pull and twist each section of pastry and lay the slices on their side, so the swirly bits are slightly exposed (see the step-by-step pictures on pages 42–43).

Brush the top of the pastry with beaten egg and sprinkle with the salt and sesame seeds. Bake in the oven for 30 minutes.

Once out of the oven, leave to cool slightly on the tray.

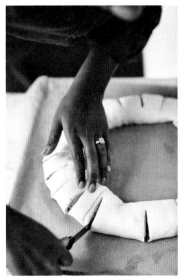

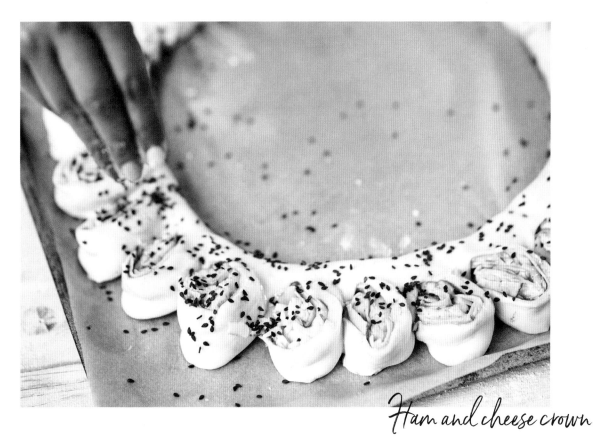

Ham and cheese crown

weekend treat, *pastry*, ham,
cheese, *twist and tear*

Lunch

Lunch often doesn't happen in our house. During the week, something else will usually take priority over my grumbling belly. On a weekend, when the kids are home, lunch ends up being squeezed between shopping trips, visits to family and ferrying the kids to appointments and activities. Life is so busy that lunch just gets lost. So, sometimes, just sometimes, I say STOP! Today, we are not going out. We don't need to see anyone. I can move that appointment. It doesn't matter that we had a big breakfast. Let's just sit and have some lunch together. Or get all hands on deck and make Sweet Potato Wraps as a family, or Piccalilli Mac 'n' Cheese, or a Samosa Pie. So here are recipes that are great to cook and eat together, before the afternoon madness begins again. Whatever which way, let's not lose lunch, even if it's only once a week.

This is in no way a replacement for steak! Steak is steak, but this recipe has every right to be honoured with the title of steak too, even though the only way it resembles steak is in the way it is cooked. Cooked in slabs, it is equally delicious, charring as it griddles. I like to serve it with a simple quick marinated halloumi dressing. I was met with scepticism when I first told my little meat-eaters that cauliflower steak was on the menu, but they were pleasantly surprised and were soon saying, 'Let's have more cauliflower.' Not bad going! This is a quick, delicious small lunch.

SERVES 4

PREP 20 MINS

COOK 20 MINS

INGREDIENTS

For the marinated halloumi
250g halloumi cheese, grated

50ml olive oil

1 tsp garlic granules

½ tsp salt

½ tsp chilli flakes

1 lemon, zest only

2 tbsp balsamic vinegar

a small handful of fresh coriander, finely chopped

For the cauliflower
1 large cauliflower

4 tbsp olive oil

salt

METHOD Start by making the quick marinated halloumi. Put the grated halloumi into a bowl, along with the oil, garlic, salt, chilli flakes, lemon zest, balsamic and coriander. Give it all a really good mix and set aside while you cook the cauliflower steaks.

To prepare the cauliflower, take off the outer leaves and most of the base stem, leaving just enough of the base that the steaks won't fall apart.

Slice the cauliflower vertically right down the centre, then slice each half vertically again, so you have 4 steak-like slices, each about 1cm thick. Of course you will have different sized steaks, as a cauliflower naturally tapers, but that's OK, there's always someone at the table who eats less! Drizzle the steaks with oil and season generously with salt.

Put a griddle pan on a high heat and fry the cauliflower on one side for 2 minutes, until you get charring on that side. Turn the steaks over and do the same on the other side. That charring will create a lovely smoky flavour.

Lower the heat to medium and cook the cauliflower until it is tender, not soft – this should only take about 6–8 minutes.

Serve up the cauliflower steaks and spoon over the marinated halloumi dressing while the cauliflower is still super-hot.

If you have any halloumi left over, pop it into a jar and keep it in the fridge for up to a week. (Or, if you're like me, you can double the recipe quantities and keep the extra batch ready in the fridge.)

CAULIFLOWER STEAK
with Marinated Halloumi

SERVES 4

PREP 15 MINS

COOK 45 MINS

Soup is one of my favourite lunches. As a teenager, I used to quite enjoy the mug variety, and to be fair, there are some fairly tasty ones out there. But there is something special about making soup from scratch at home. The only thing that doesn't like soup is my stomach, especially if the soup is thin, watery and unsatisfying. This soup is the exact opposite of that: warm and sweet, with smooth, creamy butternut squash, and hearty from the orzo pasta that is cooked in it. No unhappy stomachs here.

INGREDIENTS

1 butternut squash
(1.5kg, prepared weight
900g)

5 tbsp olive oil

2 cloves of garlic,
crushed

2.5cm fresh ginger,
peeled and chopped

1 tsp salt

1 tsp chipotle chilli flakes
(these are smoky and
hot, but if you can't find
them you can use normal
chilli flakes)

1 litre vegetable stock

100g orzo pasta

To serve

50g watercress, finely
chopped (plus extra,
unchopped, for the top)

1 lime, zest only

balsamic vinegar,
to drizzle

METHOD Prepare the squash by cutting off the top and base, so you have a stable surface at either end. Cut into 4 equal pieces and peel away the outer skin. Remove the seeds and chop the flesh into 2.5cm pieces.

Put the chopped butternut squash into a microwave-safe bowl and cover the top with clingfilm, making sure to secure the edges. Microwave the squash on high for 10 minutes. This could take a few minutes longer or a few minutes less, depending on the strength of your microwave. I would check on it at 8 minutes and then keep going in 1-minute bursts. You will know the squash is ready if, when you press it, it gives way easily. Remove the clingfilm and set the squash aside. This step will save lots of time.

Put the oil in a large saucepan on a medium heat. When it's hot, add the garlic and ginger and cook for just a few minutes, until the garlic is golden.

Add the cooked squash to the pan and stir to coat it with the garlic and ginger. Season with salt and add the chilli flakes. Pour in the vegetable stock and cook on a medium heat for about 20 minutes.

Take the pan off the heat and blend the mixture to a smooth soup, using a stick blender.

Now put the mixture back into the pan, add the orzo, and cook for about 10 minutes on a medium to low heat, until the pasta has cooked.

Take off the heat. Serve in bowls, with the watercress, lime zest and a drizzle of balsamic vinegar.

BUTTERNUT PASTA SOUP
with Watercress

The magic ingredient in this tart is a certain yeast extract spread that divides opinions: are you are lover or a hater? The fact that I've included this recipe in the book should tell you what my position is, though I'm not someone who goes in for a huge helping – just enough to tickle my tongue. I enjoy using it to cook with, for the smoky, rich, dark flavour it brings. It works so well in this cheesy frangipane tart. Perfect served with a simple salad.

SERVES 6

PREP 20 MINS

COOK 1 HOUR

INGREDIENTS

250g ready-made shortcrust pasty

2 tsp yeast extract (Marmite, Vegemite, etc.)

100g unsalted butter, softened

50g sugar

2 medium eggs

a pinch of salt

100g ground almonds

10g plain flour, plus extra for dusting

15g fresh chives, finely chopped or snipped with scissors

150g mature Cheddar cheese, grated

green salad or baked beans, to serve

METHOD Preheat the oven to 200°C/180°C fan/gas mark 6 and pop in a baking tray to heat up.

Lightly flour a worktop and roll out the pastry to about 5mm thick. Line the base and sides of a 20cm fluted, shallow, loose-bottomed tart tin, trimming the edges of the pastry with scissors, but leaving some overhang. You will cut this off later. Prick the base of the pastry with a fork and pop the lined tin into the freezer for 10 minutes. Quickly chilling the pastry stops it shrinking too much when baked. If it shrinks, where will all that lovely filling go?

Take the tart tin out of the freezer, line the pastry with baking paper and fill with baking beads (or just use uncooked rice or dried lentils).

Place the tart tin on top of the hot tray in the oven – this provides an extra really hot surface to ensure a crisp base. Bake for 20 minutes.

Take out of the oven, remove the beads (or lentils/rice), along with the paper, and place the empty tart shell back in the oven for 5 minutes. Then take it out and reduce the temperature to 180°C/160°C fan/gas mark 4.

Cover the tart base with yeast extract, using as much or as little as you wish.

To make the filling, put the butter, sugar, eggs and salt into a bowl and mix. Add the ground almonds, flour, chives and two-thirds of the grated cheese. Reserve the remaining third for the top.

Spread the mixture into the tart shell, on top of the yeast extract. This is best done using two spoons to dollop it all over – this stops the frangipane mixing with it. Level off the surface using the back of a spoon.

Sprinkle the rest of the cheese on top and bake for 35 minutes. Take out of the oven, leave to cool for 10 minutes, then trim off the edges of the pastry.

I like to serve this with a simple salad, but my kids are adamant it should be eaten with baked beans! Give both ways a go, and see what you think.

I'm not a massive fan of cold salads, but I have worked out that if I leave it out at breakfast, I can have a room temperature salad by lunchtime. But I know most normal people probably don't have salad issues like I have and you can eat yours crisp and freshly made. If I'm having a salad it must include a bit of everything: salty, sweet, crunchy, spicy, and some protein. This recipe has all those things.

SERVES 4

PREP 20 MINS

COOK 30 MINS

INGREDIENTS

For the salad

4 chicken breasts

4 tbsp olive oil

½ tsp salt

1 tbsp garam masala

100g baby spinach leaves

1 red onion, sliced

1 fresh mango, diced

1 red pepper, sliced

½ cucumber, halved and watery centre taken out, then ribboned using a potato peeler

200g crunchy coated peanuts (I like chilli ones)

For the dressing

150ml coconut cream

2 tbsp sweet mango chutney

a small handful of fresh coriander, chopped

½ a lemon, juice only

a large pinch of salt

METHOD Begin by cooking the chicken. Place a griddle pan on a high heat. Put the chicken breasts into a bowl with the oil, salt and garam masala. Get your hands in and give it all a good mix, making sure the chicken breasts are covered with the spice.

When the griddle pan is hot, add the chicken breasts and cook for 15 minutes on each side. The amount of time you need to cook the meat will largely depend on how large the breasts are. But a really good way of testing the chicken is to pierce it with a knife – any liquid that comes out should run completely clear. If it's cloudy or has specks of blood it needs cooking a bit longer.

The chicken should have dark char marks from the griddle. Take off the heat and put to one side while you prepare the salad.

Toss together the spinach leaves, red onion, mango, red pepper and cucumber and divide among 4 salad bowls. Slice the chicken into strips and put on top of the salad.

To make the dressing, mix together the coconut cream, mango chutney, chopped coriander and lemon juice. Season with a pinch of salt. Mix well and drizzle over the chicken.

Sprinkle the crunchy coated peanuts all over each bowl of salad. I love using these because they are coated in that extra jacket – they come in various flavours, but I love the chilli variety, especially on top of my salads.

CHICKEN, MANGO AND
RED PEPPER SALAD

This is as much a salad as it is a topping for crackers. It's the kind of thing that I love whipping up when I'm having an unexpected gathering in the house. A 'whack it all in a bowl and dig in' type of lunch, with creamy eggs and avocado, soft potato and salty crab, all covered with a thick dressing. Just perfect for spooning on top of some prawn crackers, straight out of the packet.

SERVES 4

PREP 20 MINS

COOK 15 MINS

INGREDIENTS

For the salad

5 eggs

2 medium potatoes, peeled (about 300g)

170g tinned shredded crabmeat, drained

1 small red onion, finely chopped

a large handful of rocket leaves

1 avocado

1 lemon, juice only

prawn crackers, to serve

For the dressing

½ tbsp Dijon mustard

1½ tbsp full-fat mayonnaise

a pinch of salt

½ tbsp honey

1 tbsp apple cider vinegar

3 tbsp olive oil

METHOD Lower your eggs gently into boiling water and simmer for 8 minutes. Rinse under cold water and, when cool to touch, peel from their shells and set aside.

Boil the potatoes in simmering salted water for 15 minutes, then drain and cool completely. Cut them into cubes and put them into a large salad bowl. Chop the eggs and add them to the bowl.

Add the crabmeat, red onion and rocket leaves, and stir through.

De-stone the avocado, then chop the flesh, place it in a small bowl and squeeze in the juice of the lemon. Stir well so that the juice coats the avocado all over. This will prevent it from going brown. In all fairness, even a brown avocado will still taste nice, but when we all know it's meant to be green, turning brown can make it unappetizing.

Stir the avocado into the salad.

Make the dressing by putting the mustard, mayonnaise, salt, honey, vinegar and olive oil into a bowl and giving it a stir. Add to the salad and stir so that everything in the salad is coated with the thick dressing.

I like to serve this salad with a huge bowl of prawn crackers, so the salad can be spooned on top of them and devoured.

This ginger rice is like the Jewish penicillin of our home. When the little ones are poorly, I like to put on a big batch of it. The rice is cooked slowly in water steeped in ginger and then finished with lots of butter. It can make you feel better when you are unwell and keep you warm when it's cold outside, and it's one of those things my body often craves, usually in the middle of the night. Sleep is for wimps anyway! When I can't sleep I pop a pot of this on the stove. If I'm having it as a proper meal I like to serve it with spiced chickpeas, piled up right in the centre of the bowl.

SERVES 4

PREP 15 MINS

COOK 1 HOUR

INGREDIENTS

For the ginger rice
100g basmati rice

750ml cold water

a pinch of salt

40g piece of fresh
ginger, peeled
and grated

200g unsalted butter,
cubed

For the spicy chickpeas
3 tbsp olive oil

1 small onion, chopped

½ tsp salt

1 tsp tomato purée

1 tomato, chopped

½ tsp chilli powder

½ tsp ground turmeric

½ tsp ground cumin

½ tsp curry powder

2 x 400g tins of
chickpeas, drained

½ a lemon

a large handful of
fresh coriander

METHOD Put a medium non-stick saucepan on a medium heat and add the rice, water, salt and grated ginger. Allow the mixture to come to the boil, being careful because if you leave it, it can boil over. (If you must walk away, turn the heat down.)

Once the rice has boiled for about 10–12 minutes, check to see if it's ready. You can tell by pressing a grain. If it's ready, it should fall apart.

Once the rice is cooked, it's time for the most important bit. Stir the rice continuously with a whisk to encourage it to break up and form a wet porridge-like consistency. Keep mixing until the mixture really begins to thicken. This can take 20–30 minutes, so you'll need to be patient.

Once the rice has thickened, lower the heat and add the butter. Whisk the butter in until it has melted. Take off the heat, pop a lid on the pan to keep the rice warm, and get on to the spicy chickpeas.

Put a large non-stick frying pan on a medium to high heat and add the oil. Once the oil is hot, add the onion, salt, tomato purée and chopped tomato, stir, then cook for about 3 minutes, until the onion has just softened.

Now add the chilli, turmeric, cumin and curry powder. If the mixture begins to stick, add a splash of water. Keep cooking on a medium to low heat for 5 minutes, to cook the spices.

Add the chickpeas and stir so they are covered in the spices. Lower the heat, add the juice of the lemon, then finely slice the rind and add to the chickpeas. Stir, then pop a lid on the pan and leave to cook for about 10 minutes on a really low heat.

Remove the lid, take the pan off the heat, and stir in the coriander.

Serve the ginger rice in bowls – it's best when it's piping hot, so just warm it through in the pan if necessary. Spoon a load of those spicy chickpeas right in the centre.

GINGER RICE with Spiced Chickpeas

PICCALILLI MACARONI CHEESE

I don't see macaroni cheese as a side dish to sit alongside the main event! For me, if I'm having macaroni cheese, it takes the leading role and it's got to be the star of the show. I like a good old classic variety at the best of times, but you know I can't help but tinker. So this is my tinkered version, which is still creamy and cheesy and mac-like, but also spiked with piquant piccalilli.

SERVES 6

PREP 20 MINS

COOK 45 MINS

INGREDIENTS
250g macaroni

350g mature Cheddar cheese, grated

1 medium egg

2 tbsp piccalilli

180g cream cheese

1 tsp onion seeds

1 tsp salt

For the crunchy topping
50g melted butter

100g dried breadcrumbs

METHOD Boil the macaroni according to the instructions on the packet. Drain in a colander, then rinse under cold running water to stop it from sticking together. Set aside.

Preheat the oven to 220°C/200°C fan/gas mark 7. Have a 23 x 23cm casserole dish or ovenproof dish at the ready.

Meanwhile put a non-stick pan on the hob and add the cheese. Keep stirring all the time while the cheese melts gently. As soon as the cheese has melted, add all the cooked pasta and mix through.

Now add the egg and stir to cook it through and mix it with the cheese mixture. This makes the dish lovely and rich.

Before adding the piccalilli, put it into a bowl and squash it with the back of a fork. Some bits can be very sharp, so you want to distribute it rather than have someone bite into a very sharp bit of cauliflower. If you are having difficulty, snip the larger bits with scissors.

Add the piccalilli to the pasta mixture along with the cream cheese, onion seeds and salt. Mix well, then pour into the casserole dish and smooth the surface so it's level.

To make the crispy topping, melt the butter. Add the breadcrumbs and mix through till the breadcrumbs are roughly coated.

Sprinkle the crumbs over the macaroni cheese and bake for 30 minutes, until the top is all golden.

CRUNCHY SPANISH OMELETTE

SERVES 4

PREP 15 MINS

COOK 15 MINS

One of my favourite things to eat when I want something quick is a Spanish omelette, which typically contains potatoes. I was about to make one recently when I realized we'd run out of potatoes (which doesn't happen often, I might add, so it caught me by surprise). Thinking on my feet, I came up with this little number. A Spanish omelette still, by name, but with the potatoes replaced by vegetable crisps! It really works.

INGREDIENTS

2 tbsp olive oil

3 spring onions, cut into 2cm lengths

½ tsp salt

125g vegetable crisps

6 medium eggs, lightly beaten

50g sliced jalapeños

50g Cheddar cheese, grated

METHOD Preheat the oven to 200°C/180°C fan/gas mark 6.

Put a medium ovenproof non-stick frying pan on a medium heat and add the oil. Add the spring onions and salt and cook for a few minutes.

Lightly crush the vegetable crisps in a bowl, then add the eggs and mix well. Turn the heat up under the frying pan and add the eggy crisp mixture. Stir the egg in the pan, scraping the edges and bringing them towards the centre, repeating this a few times. This will help the omelette cook evenly.

Put the jalapeños and cheese on top of the omelette and bake in the oven for 10–12 minutes, until golden, firm and cooked through.

Now you know what to do with spare crisps!

I've only recently really started enjoying Lebanese cuisine. It is so rich in colour and flavour and truly gets my taste buds ticking. I went to a 'Lebanese' restaurant a few years ago where everything was served with chips. Don't get me wrong, I love a chip, but what I wanted was authentic Lebanese food! When I saw chicken tikka masala on the menu I really should have left. From there, my quest for the real stuff began, and led me to this recipe. Tabbouleh is a popular salad of finely chopped herbs, tomatoes and bulgur wheat. My variation combines lots of parsley, raw vegetables, sweet pomegranates and couscous – and not a chip in sight.

SERVES 4

PREP 20 MINS

NO COOK (APART
FROM BOILING
THE KETTLE)

INGREDIENTS

250g couscous

1 tbsp butter

1 clove of garlic, crushed

2 tomatoes, deseeded
and chopped

1 carrot, grated

½ a yellow pepper,
finely diced

2 spring onions,
finely sliced

80g pomegranate seeds

6 tbsp olive oil

1 lemon, juice and zest

50g fresh flat-leaf
parsley, finely chopped

a pinch of salt

METHOD Put the couscous into a bowl, along with the butter and enough boiling water to cover the couscous by about 1cm (about 300ml). Cover with clingfilm and set aside while you prepare the rest of the ingredients.

Put the crushed garlic, tomatoes, carrot, yellow pepper, spring onions, pomegranate seeds, olive oil, lemon juice and zest, parsley and salt into a large bowl and give everything a really good mix. I like to do this using my hands – it gets all the juices released, ready for when the couscous is added, so it can absorb them all.

Uncover the couscous and fluff it up, using a fork. Add to the parsley mix and stir through.

POMEGRANATE
AND PARSLEY TABBOULEH

I only started making a Sunday lunch once my kids had a serious appreciation for a roast potato. And I must admit that our Sunday lunches are not just limited to Sundays. If we feel up for it, we make it, whatever the day. Of course, like most meals, I don't go entirely classic. The concept remains but the recipe has been adapted and changed over the years and this is our favourite combination: garlic and ginger spatchcock chicken, ghee roasties, coriander stuffing balls, turmeric greens and tomato gravy. Down with convention!

SERVES 4-5

PREP 40 MINS

COOK 1 HOUR
10 MINS

INGREDIENTS

For the chicken

1 x 1.5kg whole chicken

25ml olive oil

2 tsp ground ginger

2 tsp garlic granules

1 tsp salt

For the ghee roasties

4 large potatoes, peeled
and cut into chunks
(800g)

50g clarified butter

1 tsp salt

2 tsp baking powder

*For the coriander
stuffing balls*

30g fresh coriander

20g pine nuts

½ tsp salt

1 tsp ground coriander

40g fresh breadcrumbs

250g chicken mince

1 medium egg

3 tbsp oil, for frying

METHOD This is a long old recipe with lots of different elements, but that's what Sunday lunches are all about. Get everyone involved, share the load, and lunch will come sooner.

Start by putting the potatoes into a large saucepan of cold water. Turn the heat up to high and let the potatoes cook for 6 minutes.

Meanwhile, spatchcock the chicken by cutting it through the backbone and opening it up. Flatten the chicken by pushing down on the breast.

Drain the potatoes, then put them back into the pan with the lid on and give them a few furious shakes – this will help to rough up the edges.

Preheat the oven to 200°C/180°C fan/gas mark 6. Put the clarified butter into a large roasting tray that's big enough to fit all the potatoes. Pop the tray into the oven to heat the butter up for about 15 minutes, until it is smoking.

Put the chicken in another large roasting tray and tease your hand under the skin to create a cavity. Do this all over the chicken.

Mix together the oil, ginger, garlic and salt in a bowl. Now with your hands put this mixture under the skin of the chicken. Do this all over the chicken until you have no more mixture left. Turn the chicken skin-side down in the tray and cover with foil.

Now add the salt and baking powder to the potatoes and give them a good toss in the saucepan. Take the tray of hot butter out of the oven and gently (as the butter is hot) put the potatoes in. You should hear a really good sizzle.

Put the chicken into the oven with the tray of roasties underneath it. Cook for 30 minutes.

→|

Sunday lunch our way

spatchcock chicken, *ghee roasties,*

coriander stuffing balls, tomato gravy,

favourite family meal

For the turmeric greens
3 tbsp olive oil

2 cloves of garlic, chopped

½ tsp ground turmeric

½ tsp salt

450g green beans

For the tomato gravy
2 tbsp olive oil

1 cinnamon stick

3 cloves of garlic, chopped

1 tbsp tomato paste

3 tomatoes, chopped (about 450g)

½ tsp salt

1 tbsp tamarind paste

300ml boiling water

1 tbsp cornflour, mixed with 1 tbsp cold water

Meanwhile make the stuffing balls. Put the fresh coriander, pine nuts, salt, ground coriander, breadcrumbs, chicken mince and egg into a food processor and whiz until the mixture comes together.

Put a medium frying pan on a high heat and add the oil. Divide the stuffing mixture into 8, then wet your hands and shape each one into a smooth ball. Fry for 20 minutes, swirling the pan occasionally so they cook evenly.

After 30 minutes, take the chicken out of the oven. Take off the foil and turn the chicken around to crisp up the skin. Put back into the oven. Give the roasties a quick stir and cook them alongside the chicken for another 20 minutes.

To cook the greens, put a frying pan on a high heat and add the oil. Add the garlic and fry until brown, then add the turmeric and salt and toss in the green beans – these literally take just about 5 minutes.

Meanwhile make the gravy: put a small saucepan on the hob on a medium to high heat. Add the oil to the pan, along with the cinnamon stick and garlic. When the garlic has browned, add the tomato paste, tomatoes and salt and cook gently until the tomatoes have softened. Add the salt, tamarind and water. Let it all cook gently while the chicken cooks, allowing it to thicken. This should only take 10 minutes. When it's ready, remove the cinnamon stick.

Blitz the gravy using a stick blender, then add the cornflour and water mix and cook for another 5 minutes, giving enough time for the gravy to thicken and the flour to cook out.

Serve the meal with some warmed-up Yorkshire puddings – I always have a stash in the freezer that can be warmed up just before serving. I really hope you enjoy my alternative slightly out-there Sunday roast.

If I have not already professed my hatred for cold salads, this is another excuse for me to moan about them – and to do something about it, too. I love the combination of a Niçoise: potatoes, anchovies, tuna, olives and Parmesan. Just delicious, but even better when the same classic ingredients are warmed right up, as I've done here!

SERVES 4

PREP 20 MINS

COOK 30-35 MINS

INGREDIENTS

For the salad

8 new potatoes
(about 375g)

4 eggs

2 x 170g tins of tuna,
drained

5 cherry tomatoes,
quartered

115g green beans, cut
into 2.5cm pieces

1 small red onion,
thinly sliced

100g pitted black olives,
halved

3 anchovies,
chopped finely

150g Parmesan shavings

For the dressing

5 tbsp olive oil

2 cloves of garlic,
crushed and chopped

2 tbsp balsamic vinegar

1 tsp dried parsley

2 tsp dried chives

½ tsp salt

METHOD Boil the new potatoes in simmering salted water for 15–20 minutes. Drain and cool, then cut into quarters.

Lower your eggs gently into boiling water and simmer for 8 minutes. Rinse under cold water and, when cool to touch, peel from their shells and cut into quarters.

Put the potatoes, eggs, tuna, tomatoes, beans, red onion, olives and anchovies into a 20 x 30cm ovenproof dish. Preheat the oven to 200°C/ 180°C fan/gas mark 6.

To make the dressing, put the oil, garlic, vinegar, parsley, chives and salt into a bowl and mix well. Add the dressing to the baking dish and give the whole thing a good stir, making sure everything is coated well.

Put the Parmesan shavings on top and bake in the oven for about 15 minutes. This is just enough time for all the loveliness in the dish to warm through, but also for the cheese to melt and crisp up on top.

This is best served straight away. I like it with a glass of fizzy water and some trashy afternoon telly.

SAMOSA PIE

SERVES 8

PREP 30 MINUTES,
PLUS COOLING

COOK 1 HOUR
45 MINUTES

I could eat samosas at any time of any day! With their crisp pastry and warm spicy filling they are like little parcels of joy. Now I've turned my all-time favourite street food snack into a picnic pie, still with an aromatic meaty filling and crisp shell, but made with hot water crust pastry.

INGREDIENTS

For the filling

5 tbsp olive oil

3 small onions,
finely diced

1½ tsp salt

1 tsp ground ginger

1 tbsp garlic granules

1 tbsp cumin seeds

2 tsp chilli flakes

500g lamb mince

500g potatoes, peeled
and diced into
small cubes

200g frozen peas

2 tbsp cornflour

a large handful of fresh
coriander, chopped

For the hot water pastry

265g plain flour

55g strong bread flour,
plus extra for dusting

½ tsp salt

1 tsp ground turmeric

135ml hot water

65g vegetable fat

1 egg, beaten, for glazing

METHOD For the filling, put the oil in a large saucepan on a medium heat. When it's hot, add the onions and salt. Cook for about 5 minutes until soft and translucent, then add the ginger, garlic, cumin seeds and chilli flakes and cook for a few minutes. Add the mince and cook until browned.

Stir in the potatoes, then reduce the heat to low to medium, cover the pan and cook for 20 minutes, until the potatoes are soft. Add the frozen peas and cook them through.

Stir in the cornflour – this will help to thicken any juices left at the bottom of the pan. Take off the heat and stir in the chopped coriander. Set aside to cool completely.

Preheat the oven to 200°C/180°C fan/gas mark 6. Have ready a 20cm round loose-bottomed cake tin.

To make the pastry, put the two flours into a bowl with the salt and turmeric. Mix well, then make a well in the centre.

Put the water and fat into a pan and heat until the fat has melted. Pour into the well in the flour, then mix using a palette knife. As soon as the dough is cool enough to handle, get your hands in and bring it all together.

Lightly dust a work surface. Set aside one-third of the dough for the top, and roll out the rest to fit the base and sides of the tin, with some overhang. Line the tin with the pastry, leaving the excess hanging over the edges. Fill the pastry-lined tin with the samosa filling.

Roll out the rest of the pastry to make the top. Brush the inner ring of pastry above the filling with beaten egg and put the lid on top, pushing it down snug to the filling. Press the edges to thoroughly seal, then cut off the overhang and fold the remaining cut edge back into the tin. Pleat the edges as you wish, brush with beaten egg and pierce a hole in the centre so steam can escape. Bake in the oven for 1 hour.

Leave to cool completely in the tin, then remove and cut into slices.

SARDINE ARRABIATA

When you have a young family, a growing family, or just a busy life, sometimes it's the simplest recipes that are the most rewarding. Arrabbiata is a classic tomato sauce that has been a staple in our home for years now, but it evolves often, and this sardine version is our latest favourite go-to after the kids' swimming lessons.

SERVES 4

PREP 15 MINS

COOK 20 MINS

INGREDIENTS

300g dried spaghetti

2 x 125g tins of sardines in olive oil

6 cloves of garlic, finely chopped

1 tsp tomato purée

1 tsp salt

2 tsp chilli flakes

2 tbsp capers

500g passata

a large handful of fresh coriander, chopped

METHOD Cook the spaghetti according to the instructions on the packet, then drain and set aside.

This is the quickest sauce ever. Be prepared to eat very soon! Put a large non-stick pan on a medium heat. Open the cans of sardines and take out the fish, then add the oil to the pan. No sense in using oil out of a bottle if you have loads in the can with the fish!

Add the garlic to the oil and cook until it is golden.

Add the tomato purée, salt and chilli flakes. Cook just for a few minutes, then add the sardines and capers and cook them through, breaking up the sardines.

Add the passata and let it simply warm through for about 5 minutes, giving it time to infuse with everything else.

Stir in the spaghetti, along with the coriander. You are ready to eat. I told you it was quick!

There's a lot of food that I never discovered until I was a mother. The need to explore and feed my children different things has led me down many an unfamiliar supermarket aisle. But we are all the better for it. Gnocchi was one of the first things my son tried, and while he wasn't the biggest fan to begin with, over time it has become a staple in our house. These gnocchi are made with a mixture of potatoes and rice flour and tossed in a fragrant sesame pesto. What's not to love?

SERVES 4-5

PREP 40 MINS

COOK 30 MINS

INGREDIENTS

For the gnocchi
700g large potatoes
150g rice flour, plus extra for dusting
1 tsp salt
3 medium egg yolks
6 tbsp olive oil, for frying

For the sesame pesto (makes 250ml)
50g sesame seeds
50g Parmesan cheese
80g fresh basil
150ml olive oil
3 cloves of garlic

METHOD Peel the potatoes and chop them into chunks. The smaller the chunks, the less time they will take to cook. Put them into a pan of cold water, bring to the boil, and boil on high for 20 minutes, or until the potatoes are tender. Drain, then mash using a ricer or a potato masher and leave to cool completely.

While the potatoes are cooking, make the pesto. Put the sesame seeds, Parmesan, basil, oil and garlic into a food processor and blitz to a smooth pesto-like paste.

Once the mashed potatoes are cooled, mix in the rice flour and salt. Add the egg yolks and mix to a smooth firm dough.

Dust a work surface with rice flour. Quarter the dough, then take each quarter and roll it into a sausage shape. One at a time, cut each sausage shape into 2cm pieces.

To cook the gnocchi, place a large saucepan of water on the hob on a high heat. When the water comes to the boil, turn the heat down to medium and drop in the gnocchi. You will know they are ready when they float to the surface. Remove them from the pan with a slotted spoon and set aside.

Now take a large non-stick frying pan and place it on a high heat. Add 3 tablespoons of oil, and when it's hot, drop in half the gnocchi and fry until they are crisp around the edges.

Once the gnocchi are crisp, remove the pan from the heat and stir through a few tablespoons of pesto. Tip everything on to a plate and keep warm.

Wipe out the pan with kitchen paper, then add the remaining 3 table-spoons of oil and repeat with the rest of the gnocchi and pesto.

RICE-FLOUR GNOCCHI
with Sesame Pesto

SERVES 4

PREP **20 MINS,**
INCLUDING
MARINATING

COOK **5 MINS**

Ceviche, the process of 'cooking' fish in lemon juice or something acidic, sounds a little out there, but it is delicious and delicate. I wanted to do things differently, so I'm using the same pickling process but with crisp fresh radish. Its vivid colour and delicious light flavour looks and tastes great on top of some sourdough and avocado.

INGREDIENTS

1 x 200g pack
of radishes

4 limes, juice only,
reserving 2 tbsp for
the avocados

2 tsp caster sugar

1 small red onion,
thinly sliced

2 tbsp olive oil

a large handful of fresh
dill, finely chopped

2 medium avocados

4 slices of sourdough or
wholemeal bread,
toasted

a pinch of freshly ground
black pepper

METHOD Slice the radishes into thin slices as best you can, using a sharp knife. Put them into a bowl.

Put the lime juice, sugar, red onion, olive oil and dill into a smaller bowl. Stir together, then add to the radishes and mix gently. This only needs 10 minutes to infuse.

Meanwhile, toast the sourdough.

Mash the avocado with the reserved 2 tablespoons of lime juice, to prevent any browning. Spread the toast with the avocado and add a sprinkling of black pepper.

Drain the radishes through a colander to remove any excess lime juice, and place slices of radish and onion on top of the avocado.

RADISH CEVICHE
with Avocado and Toasted Sourdough

SERVES 4

PREP 25 MINS

COOK 30 MINS

INGREDIENTS

*For the sweet
potato wraps*
1 large sweet potato
(382g)

½ tsp salt

150g plain flour, plus
extra for dusting

For the sweetcorn relish
1 clove of garlic, crushed

½ a small red onion,
finely chopped

1 small tomato, deseeded
and chopped

1 small green chilli,
chopped

1 lime, zest and juice

a handful of fresh
coriander, finely
chopped

1 x 326g tin of
sweetcorn, drained

For the chicken
3 tbsp olive oil

500g chicken thighs,
sliced

a pinch of salt

120g sandwich pickle

I keep my troops up and about on wraps. They're versatile, portable and can be filled with a wide array of different things: that's why we love them so much in our house. These are a personal favourite, for days when I don't want to pull them out of a packet. The kind of thing you reserve to really show the kids what you're made of. Made with sweet potatoes, they are delicious filled with simple grilled chicken thigh slices and zesty sweetcorn relish.

METHOD To make the sweet potato wraps, put the sweet potato into the microwave for 8–10 minutes on high.

While the potato is cooking, make the relish. Put the garlic, onion, tomato, chilli, lime zest and juice, coriander and sweetcorn into a bowl and give it all a good stir. Cover and leave aside.

Take care when handling the sweet potato, as it will be very hot. Use oven gloves or just let it sit with the microwave door open for 5 minutes. When it's cool enough to handle, cut it in half lengthways and scoop out the flesh. You need 250g.

Put the sweet potato flesh into a bowl with the salt and flour and mix to bring the dough together.

Divide the mixture into 4 equal parts. Dust a work surface with flour and roll out one piece of the dough into a large circle. Do the same to the other 3.

Put a large non-stick frying pan on the hob and turn the heat up to high. Dry-fry the wraps for 1–2 minutes on each side. You will know they are ready when they have large brown patches where they have caught on the pan. Pile the wraps on a plate and cover with foil while you fry the chicken.

Using the same pan, just wipe off any excess flour or burnt bits with kitchen paper. Place back on the hob on a high heat.

Add the olive oil and, when the oil is hot, add the chicken pieces and cook for a few minutes until they have cooked through – this will take about 5 minutes. Season with salt and add the sandwich pickle. Keep cooking on a high heat until any moisture has evaporated and the chicken is sticky – this can take another 5 minutes.

Time to assemble. Take a wrap, fill it with chicken and add lots of relish on top. Roll and go!

SWEET POTATO WRAPS
with Chicken and Sweetcorn Relish

Now that our supermarkets are broadening their horizons, I recently found myself arriving home with frozen edamame beans. But what to do with frozen edamame? My first reaction was to cook something curry-related, but though it was delicious I still felt unsatisfied. Edamame beans are so fresh and green that they don't need to be spoiled, just enhanced and enjoyed, and this simple salad does exactly that, by topping them with a delicious teriyaki tofu.

SERVES 4

PREP 20 MINS, PLUS MARINATING

COOK 15 MINS

INGREDIENTS

For the teriyaki tofu
2 x 280g blocks of extra-firm tofu

3 tbsp dark soy sauce

2 tbsp rice vinegar

2 tsp sesame oil

2 tbsp honey

2 tsp ground ginger

vegetable oil, for frying

For the salad
500g frozen edamame beans, defrosted

1 large carrot, grated

2 tbsp light soy sauce

2 tbsp rice vinegar

1 tsp ground ginger

1 tbsp black sesame seeds

2 spring onions, finely sliced

METHOD Slice the tofu into 1cm-thick pieces and place in a bowl. Add the soy sauce, vinegar, sesame oil, honey and ginger. I like to leave this for a few hours in the fridge. If I'm having it for lunch I will prep this just after breakfast, giving it a few hours to marinate before lunchtime.

Before cooking the tofu, make the edamame salad by putting the beans into a bowl with the grated carrot, soy sauce, vinegar, ginger and sesame seeds. Mix, then set aside while you fry the tofu.

Put a medium non-stick pan on the hob and turn it up to a medium heat. Add a few tablespoons of vegetable oil and, as soon as the oil is hot, add the slices of tofu (reserving the marinade). Fry until the edges are sticky and have caught a little. This should only take a few minutes on each side. Take the tofu out and set it aside on a plate. Add the marinade to the pan and cook for 5 minutes, until the sauce has reduced. Put the tofu back into the pan to warm up again.

Serve the edamame topped with the slices of tofu and sprinkled with spring onions.

Sides and sharers

Whenever my husband and I go out to eat and a menu is placed in front of us, we both always turn straight to the section labelled sides. To me, those little tasters of deliciousness can be just what I fancy. Or the one thing that makes all the difference to the main dish. They are also the only part of a meal that comes with unwritten permission for sharing – there to be tucked into, mixed and matched, and ultimately wolfed down by everyone. Spread across a table, sides can bring people together as we mmmm and aaaah over the little plates, hands and wrists crossing as we reach for the best ones. So here's a chapter full of them, to share with others or to keep all for yourself if that's what you feel like. Pass the sides!

MAKES **48**
BISCUITS

PREP **30 MINS**,
PLUS CHILLING

COOK **30 MINS**

INGREDIENTS

For the cheese biscuits
120g plain flour, plus
extra for dusting

120g unsalted butter,
cubed

120g smoked cheese,
grated finely

½ tsp mustard powder

1 tsp garlic granules

½ tsp onion salt

1 tsp sugar

For the tomato jam
6 tomatoes
(about 540g)

2 tbsp olive oil

1 whole star anise

1 small onion,
finely chopped

2 heaped tbsp brown
sugar

½ tsp salt

1 tsp tomato purée

3 tbsp Worcestershire
sauce

Cheese biscuits are a staple for anyone with small kids, and they have been my saving grace at many a crucial moment. When I feel my blood-pressure drop, and my feet haven't touched the ground, that leftover cheese biscuit is like the light in the abyss that is my handbag. Even now they're bigger, my kids still have more than a fondness – rather an addiction – to these savoury delights. So this is a recipe they will fully appreciate: a salty cheesy biscuit with a sweet tomato jam.

METHOD Begin with the biscuits. Put the flour and butter into a bowl, and rub with your fingertips until the mixture resembles breadcrumbs. If it's easier, pulse everything together in a processor. Mix in the cheese, mustard, garlic, onion salt and sugar. Bring the dough together with your hands, then flatten, wrap in clingfilm and chill for 15 minutes in the fridge.

To make the jam, cut slits in the tomato skins and place the tomatoes in a bowl. Pour in boiling water to submerge the tomatoes, then cover with clingfilm and leave for 10 minutes. This makes it easier to remove the skins.

Meanwhile preheat the oven to 180°C/160°C fan/gas mark 4. Line a baking tray or two with baking paper.

Dust a work surface lightly with flour. Take the dough out of the fridge, unwrap and roll out to 5mm thick. Using a round 4cm cutter, cut out the biscuits and pop them on the trays. Gather any offcuts into a ball, roll out flat and cut out more rounds. Keep doing this until the dough is all used up.

Using a fork, pierce a few holes in the top of each biscuit, to allow steam to escape and stop them puffing up. Bake for 12–15 minutes, until the biscuits are golden and crisp on top. If you are putting a tray on a lower shelf, it will need an extra 3–4 minutes.

Back to the jam. Remove the tomatoes from the hot water and peel away the skins. Roughly chop the tomatoes and set aside.

Pop a non-stick saucepan on a medium heat and add the oil. When it's hot, add the star anise and onion and cook for 5 minutes, until the onion is soft. Now add the sugar, salt and tomato purée and stir until the sugar has dissolved. Add the chopped tomatoes and Worcestershire sauce and cook on a low to medium heat until any liquid has evaporated and the jam is sticky – this should only take 10 minutes.

Once the biscuits are baked, leave them on the tray for a few minutes, then remove them to cool on a rack. Eat them with the still-warm jam.

CHEESE BISCUITS
with Tomato Jam

SERVES 4

PREP 15 MINS

COOK 10 MINS

Gone are the days of boiling broccoli to within an inch of its life. I love broccoli in a curry, but not when it is unrecognizable after being stewed for an hour. I can't see the point in eating green veg if you can't hear them in your head when you are crunching on them! Baking broccoli is very easy, and you can flavour it so many ways. I love it with a few gentle spices tossed through, baked simply, with some toasted almonds to top it off.

INGREDIENTS

2 large heads of broccoli, florets removed from the stem

30ml olive oil

3 cloves of garlic, peeled and chopped

1 tsp salt

1 tsp chilli flakes

1 tsp cumin seeds

1 tsp ground coriander

2 tbsp balsamic vinegar

1 lemon, zest only

50g almond flakes

METHOD Preheat the oven to 220°C/200°C fan/gas mark 7.

Cut each broccoli floret in half, and cut any larger florets into quarters. Scatter the florets on a baking tray, so they are evenly arranged.

Make the dressing by mixing together the oil, garlic, salt, chilli flakes, cumin seeds and coriander in a bowl. Drizzle two-thirds of the dressing over the broccoli and use your hands to make sure it is all coated. Pop the baking tray into the oven for 4 minutes.

Add the balsamic vinegar to the remaining third of the dressing, along with the lemon zest. Stir, then drizzle the mixture over the broccoli, making sure it is all coated.

Scatter the almonds on top and bake for another 4 minutes.

Serve alongside whatever you want. But I quite like a massive bowl of this sometimes and nothing else.

BAKED BROCCOLI

SERVES 4

PREP 20 MINS

COOK 20 MINS

Kati rolls are a common street food back in my parents' homeland, where they are often filled with grilled meats and piquant salads. Keen to make a vegetarian version of the delicious kati roll at home, here I've filled a crisp egg-fried tortilla with creamy spinach and paneer. It makes a great snack or something to eat on the side. There is something about that vibrant green that makes me pleased it's not in smoothie form!

INGREDIENTS

*For the spinach
and paneer*
3 tbsp olive oil

226g block of paneer
cheese, cut into
1cm cubes

150g spinach leaves

150ml water

4 cloves of garlic,
chopped

1 tsp cumin seeds

½ tsp chilli flakes

½ tsp salt

For the kati rolls
olive oil, for frying

2 eggs

a pinch of salt

4 small tortilla wraps

METHOD Put a non-stick saucepan on a medium heat with 2 tablespoons of the oil. As soon as the oil is hot, add the paneer and fry for 5 minutes, stirring occasionally. You want to colour the paneer as much as possible.

Put the spinach leaves and water into a blender and whiz to a smooth paste. Add a splash more water if needed, to blend smoothly.

Take the paneer out of the pan with a slotted spoon and set aside. Add the remaining tablespoon of oil and the garlic to the pan and cook for a minute, until the garlic is light brown.

Add the green mixture, along with the cumin seeds, chilli flakes and salt, and cook on a medium heat for 5 minutes, until some of the water from around the edge has reduced and the mixture has thickened.

Add the paneer to the pan and mix well, making sure all the cheese is covered in green. Pop a lid on the pan and leave on a low heat while you make the rolls.

Put a small frying pan on a high heat and add a good glug of oil, enough to cover the base.

Break the eggs into a very shallow bowl with the salt and lightly whisk – the bowl needs to be flat enough to be able to dunk the tortillas. Dip a tortilla into the egg mixture, making sure to cover it all over. Get it straight into the frying pan. The oil should be hot enough to really create a sizzle. Cook for just 30 seconds, then turn it over and cook on the other side. Now cook the other 3 tortillas the same way.

To serve, add the paneer mixture to the centre of a hot crispy tortilla, and roll up. Not like a burrito, but the way a kid would make a roll for the first time. If you don't have cheese falling out one end, you're doing it wrong!

SPINACH AND PANEER KATI ROLLS

The flavour of Indian pickle is unique and really rather strong. I eat curries with my hands, so if there is pickle involved in that meal, my nose will know for at least another week! I couldn't eat pickle during my first pregnancy because I found the smell horrific, and if my husband had eaten it I asked him to sleep the other way round so that I couldn't smell it on his breath. I would rather smell his feet, it was that bad to me! Poor man. Nearly twelve years later, I still struggle a tiny bit, but I can eat it. I love using jarred pickles as an ingredient and they work really well with mushrooms. As the crispy bread is the carrier, I don't have to live with a lingering smell on my hands.

SERVES 8

PREP 20 MINS

COOK 30 MINS

INGREDIENTS

8 slices of white bread

125g garlic butter, melted (if you can't find garlic butter to buy, melt 125g of butter and mix in 2 crushed cloves of garlic)

a pinch of salt

For the pickle mushrooms
3 tbsp olive oil (plus any extra leftover garlic butter from the bread)

1 red onion, thinly sliced

1 tbsp tomato purée

a pinch of salt

1½ tbsp Indian lime pickle

700g mushrooms, thinly sliced (use a mixture of types if you like)

METHOD Preheat the oven to 200°C/180°C fan/gas mark 6. Have a baking tray or two at the ready.

Cut each slice of bread in half lengthways, to make 2 smaller rectangles of bread. Take a rolling pin and flatten the bread out as much as you can. Brush all over with the garlic butter, being generous. Pop the slices of bread on to the baking tray and sprinkle with salt.

Bake in the oven for 15–20 minutes, until they are crisp and golden. Turn them around halfway through, and keep checking so they don't burn.

Meanwhile, make the pickle mushrooms. Put a large pan on a high heat and add the oil and any leftover garlic butter from the bread. As soon as the oil is hot, add the onion, tomato purée, a sprinkle of salt and the lime pickle. Cook until the onion is just soft and the pieces of lime are breaking down.

Add the mushrooms and stir them into the onion mixture, then cook on a medium heat until they have really reduced. As soon as you can see the moisture from the mushrooms in the base of the pan, turn the heat to high and allow the liquid to evaporate, keeping a close eye as the mushrooms will catch quickly once the liquid has gone. This could take about 10 minutes.

Take the toasted bread out of the oven and serve 2 pieces per person, alongside the hot pickle mushrooms.

CRISPY BREAD
with Pickle Mushrooms

PESTO PRAWNS

SERVES 4

PREP 10 MINS

COOK 10 MINS

These are so simple to make. Succulent prawns, covered with a pesto coating, then baked in the oven. With a pot of mayonnaise beside them for dipping, it's hard not to eat the lot. (I can vouch for that, because I ate the lot.)

INGREDIENTS

2 x 180g packs of large raw king prawns, with no shells

1 egg yolk

a pinch of salt

75g ground almonds

1½ tbsp plain flour

4 fresh basil leaves

1½ tbsp finely grated Parmesan cheese

2 tsp garlic granules

spray oil

METHOD Pat the prawns dry and remove any excess moisture. Pop them into a bowl and add the egg yolk. Stir it around, making sure all the prawns are coated. Season with a pinch of salt and set aside.

Put the ground almonds, flour, basil leaves, Parmesan and garlic granules into a small food processor and process until the mixture is an even crumb.

Preheat the oven to 220°C/200°C fan/gas mark 7. Grease a baking tray with a little spray oil and have it ready to put the prawns on.

Put the pesto crumb mixture on a plate. One by one, coat each prawn with the crumb mixture, making sure the whole prawn is covered and packing the coating tightly around each one. Place the prawns on the prepared tray.

Spray the prawns with a light coating of the spray oil and bake in the oven for 10 minutes. Halfway through the cooking, turn the tray around. The outside of the prawns should be light golden brown and the inside plump and cooked. Serve on a big platter.

LENTIL FRITTERS

Believe it or not, these light fritters made with pulsed lentils are another one of my favourite things to eat with a cup of tea. They are lightly spiced and fragrant and work really well with a simple English breakfast. A handy thing to do is to make a load of them at once, eat as many as you can, then freeze the rest. They can be simply reheated in the oven from frozen.

MAKES **40 FRITTERS**

PREP **15 MINS,**
PLUS SOAKING

COOK **20 MINS**

INGREDIENTS

120g red split lentils

1 tsp salt

2 red chillies, finely chopped (remove the seeds if you want it less spicy)

½ a red onion, finely chopped

1 tsp ground coriander

15g fresh coriander, finely chopped

1 medium egg

100g gram (chickpea) flour

500ml oil

METHOD Begin by soaking the lentils for a minimum of 3 hours in cold water. If you want, you can soak them the day before. I like to tick things off and get them done so they don't escape my sieve-like memory.

Drain the lentils and put in a food processor. Pulse to a smooth paste.

Transfer the lentil paste to a bowl and add the salt, chillies, onion, ground coriander and fresh coriander. Mix well. Mix in the egg, then the gram flour. The mixture should be like a thick cake batter.

Put a medium saucepan on a high heat and fill about one-third full with oil. Using a medium pan will mean frying the fritters in several smaller batches, but it also means less oil is needed.

If you are someone who uses a cooking thermometer, your oil needs to be 170°C. If you don't have one, just drop in a little bit of the mix. When it rises to the top, the oil is ready. When the oil is hot enough, turn the heat down to medium and add the batter 1 teaspoon at a time, making sure not to overcrowd the pan. Keep moving the fritters around as they fry gently. They will only take about 5 minutes. Pop them on to a plate lined with kitchen paper to drain off any excess oil.

Repeat until you have used up all the batter. You will probably need to do about 4 batches. If the oil has cooled between batches, just turn up the heat until it is hot enough again.

Enjoy these with your favourite dip or drink – mine is a good cup of builder's tea. To each his own.

MAKES **8 BAGS**

PREP **20 MINS**

NO COOK

Chaat is a very popular street food in Bangladesh, where the streets are lined with market vendors on tiny stalls that waft big aromas. Chaat is often a combination of crispy fried noodles topped with fresh onions, chillies, coriander and many other delights. It varies from vendor to vendor, so part of the joy is in trying every single one, each different in its own way, with the vendor's special twist. This is my version, made in the comfort of my home. It is the kind of thing I like to take on a picnic to eat after a long bike ride, or simply serve at a gathering. Best of all, it's mixed and served in the tortilla packet, so no plates or washing-up needed!

INGREDIENTS

1 large red onion

5 large chillies

250g salted peanuts

200g ready-fried onions

a large handful of fresh coriander

8 individual bags (approx. 30g each) of salted tortilla chips

For the mint sauce
200g full-fat mayonnaise

1 tsp garlic powder

1 tsp dried mint

2 tbsp whole milk

For the tamarind sauce
200g ketchup

4 tsp tamarind paste

METHOD This recipe really is all about prep. Best of all is that each person makes their own, so that's all that needs doing and everyone else can do the rest. But that's also the joy of a snack like this. It's about digging in!

Depending on where you are eating this, either pop the prepared bits into a lunchbox, ready to go, or into serving bowls ready to eat.

Finely dice the onion and pop it into a bowl. I really don't like massive chunks of raw onion.

Chop the chillies, and take the seeds out if you like it less spicy. I like to keep the seeds in and again make sure it is chopped up finely. I certainly don't like massive chunks of chilli in my mouth, unlike my husband!

Pop the peanuts and fried onions into 2 separate bowls. Chop the coriander roughly and place it in another bowl.

For the mint sauce, mix together the mayonnaise, garlic, mint and milk. I like to use a squeezy bottle (an old ketchup bottle, washed, that I re-use all the time) – it just makes it easier to get the sauce into the bag. But if you don't have one, a bowl is fine.

Do the same with the ketchup and tamarind – mix together and pop them into a bottle or bowl.

Now, to eat these, there is no hard and fast rule. I like doing it in the order listed here, but you can go any which way. To start, crush the tortilla chips while the packets are still sealed. Turn the packets on their side and cut the sides open. Now get involved – sprinkle over the onion, chilli, peanuts, crispy onions, coriander, mint sauce and tamarind sauce.

Use a disposable fork to give it all a mix, go in, and when you're finished bin the lot! Street food on the sofa.

CHAAT IN A BAG

HUMMUS THREE WAYS

I go through bouts of eating a lot of hummus, to the point where I can't even look at it any more! But after a day or two off the stuff, I usually go straight back to my hummus frenzy. We tend to use it all through the week, especially in sandwiches for the kids' lunches, and I also like to make it a focal part of a meal, so I have developed 3 different recipes for making it. I figure if you love something so much, you may as well eat it every which way. So here is a cauliflower hummus, a burnt garlic hummus, and a pickled ginger and butter bean variety, all great served with a load of crudités and breads of your choice.

MAKES **8**

PREP **20 MINS**

COOK **5 MINS**

INGREDIENTS

For cauliflower hummus

300g pack of cauliflower rice (or 300g florets)

2 tbsp cream cheese

1 tbsp tahini

1 tbsp olive oil

a large pinch of salt

2 tbsp lemon juice

a large handful of fresh chives, chopped (keep a little for the top)

For pickled ginger and butter bean hummus

1 x 200g tin of butter beans, drained (125g drained weight)

1 tbsp pickled ginger, plus extra for the top

a large pinch of salt

1 tbsp tahini

4 tbsp olive oil

METHOD

For the cauliflower hummus

Put the cauliflower rice into a microwave-safe bowl and add a splash of water. Cover with clingfilm and steam for 3 minutes on high. If you are using florets, cook them for 5 minutes.

Drain off any excess moisture and pop the cauliflower rice into a food processor, along with the cream cheese, tahini, oil, salt and lemon juice. Whiz to a smooth paste. If it needs loosening, add a little water.

Add most of the chopped chives and give it another blast just for 1 second, to combine. Pop it into a bowl and sprinkle the reserved chives on top.

For the ginger hummus

Put the butter beans, ginger, salt, tahini and oil into a food processor and whiz to a paste. If the mixture is not smooth enough, add a little water to loosen. Pop it into a bowl and scatter some extra bits of finely sliced pickled ginger on top.

For burnt garlic hummus

1 clove of garlic, unpeeled

1 x 200g tin of chickpeas, drained (125g drained weight)

1 tsp ground cumin

a large pinch of salt

1 tbsp tahini

4 tbsp olive oil

1 tsp paprika, plus a little extra for the top

To serve

warm breads and crudités

For the burnt garlic hummus

Burn the garlic on a gas flame until the skin is charred and completely black. You could do the same thing with a blowtorch, by placing the garlic on a baking tray. The skin will be burnt, but that's what gives this hummus its distinct flavour.

Put the garlic into a food processor with the chickpeas, cumin, salt, tahini, oil and paprika and whiz to a smooth paste. If the mixture is too thick, add a little water until it's the right consistency. Pop it into a bowl and sprinkle with more paprika.

Serve your choice of hummus with warm breads and crudités.

Prawn toast is the first thing we always order when we get a takeaway in. They're a little bit greasy (okay, a lot greasy!), but I love them, with the soft prawns and fried sesame seeds. I quite like making them at home too, but good prawns are not the cheapest, so I have created a more affordable alternative using chicken breast. This means I can lather on the chicken and get a really good thick layer without having to make just a little go a long way.

MAKES **28 TOASTS**

PREP **20 MINS**

COOK **7 MINS**

INGREDIENTS

450g chicken mince

1 medium egg

a large handful of
fresh coriander

1 tsp chilli flakes

1 tsp ground coriander

1 tsp salt

1 clove of garlic

7 slices of white bread,
crusts still on

75g white sesame seeds

25g black sesame seeds

300ml vegetable oil,
to shallow-fry

METHOD Make the chicken mix by putting the mince, egg, fresh coriander, chilli flakes, ground coriander, salt and garlic into a food processor. Blitz to a smooth paste and transfer to a bowl. Turning this into a paste will make spreading it a lot easier.

Lay out the slices of bread and lather each one with an even layer of the chicken paste.

Put both types of sesame seed on a flat plate wide enough to fit the bread, and mix them together well. Press all the slices of bread, chicken side down, on to the sesame seeds.

Cut each slice of bread on the diagonal, criss-cross, and then again, so you have little triangles. Now these need to be shallow-fried, so put a medium frying pan on the hob and turn the heat to medium. Drop a stray sesame seed into the oil, and if it floats up to the surface the oil is ready.

Put the toasts in, chicken side down, and fry for 5 minutes. Then turn them over and fry for 2 minutes on the other side. Take out and drain on kitchen paper. I challenge you not to polish off the lot!

NOT PRAWN TOAST

MAKES 28
POTSTICKERS

PREP 30 MINS

COOK 20 MINS

My boys love eating dumplings, of any variety. Steamed, fried, but especially potstickers. Keen to avoid making the pastry myself, I have been on many a quest for dumpling wrappers. But they are not that easy to find. So I have found an ingenious way of creating the wrappers using filo pastry, which can be bought in all supermarkets. I don't stick to rules and I'm not about to start now. The fillings can vary, but I like to keep it simple, and these are just that, fragrant with lemon and parsley.

INGREDIENTS

1 x 270g packet of
ready-made filo pastry

spray oil

4 tbsp olive oil

For the prawn filling
280g raw prawns,
with no shells

15g fresh parsley,
roughly chopped

1 lemon, zest and
2 tbsp juice

½ tsp salt

2 tsp cornflour

For the sweet soy dip
60ml dark soy sauce

60ml rice vinegar

2 tsp sesame oil

2 tsp caster sugar

1 spring onion,
finely chopped

2.5cm fresh ginger,
peeled and grated

METHOD Start by cutting out pastry rounds with a 10cm round cutter. Pile the pastry rounds up and pop them into a zip-lock bag while you make the filling.

Put the prawns into a food processor with the parsley, lemon zest and juice, salt and cornflour. Blend to a smooth paste, then transfer to a bowl.

Have a bowl of water ready alongside your bag of pastry. Take 2 rounds of pastry out at a time. Using the lightest touch, brush water all over 1 round, then put the other round on top and stick them together. Now place half a teaspoon of the prawn filling in the centre.

I could give you instructions for an elaborate pleating method. But just wet your hands, wet the edges of the pastry, and pinch it together in the centre. The wet pastry will stick together.

Pop the dumpling on a tray, then make the rest.

To steam them, put a pan (make sure it has a lid that fits) on the hob and add about 2.5cm of water. Pop a colander on top and spray it lightly with oil to stop the dumplings sticking when you add them. As soon as the water boils and the steam rises, put the dumplings into the colander, pop the lid on and steam for 3 minutes. Do this in batches, until you have steamed them all.

Place a large wok on a high heat and add the olive oil. Pop the dumplings in – again, you may have to do this in batches. Fry the dumplings until they literally stick to the pan and char. They just need frying on one side, like traditional dumplings. Repeat until they are all cooked.

To make the dip, simply put all the ingredients into a small bowl. Mix and you are good to get dipping.

PRAWN POTSTICKERS
with Sweet Soy Dip

SERVES 6-8

PREP 40 MINS

COOK 35 MINS

Smoked fish and rare steak are two things my nan will never understand (this from a woman who eats fermented fish!), but I love smoked mackerel, especially as a pâté. It's delicious paired with my spicy sweet chutney and freshly baked choux, perfect for plonking in the middle of the table and saying go for it. Everyone has their own preferred pâté-to-chutney ratio: I'm a half-and-half. I wonder what Nan would have?

INGREDIENTS

For the choux
200ml cold water
4 tsp caster sugar
85g unsalted butter, plus extra for greasing
a pinch of salt
115g plain flour, sifted
3 medium eggs, beaten

For the mackerel pâté
400g smoked mackerel, skin removed
8 tbsp Greek yoghurt
100g butter, melted
a pinch of salt
½ tsp freshly ground black pepper

For the pineapple chutney
1 x 435g tin of pineapple chunks, drained
1 large handful of fresh coriander, stalks included
2 small green chillies
1 lime, juice and zest
a pinch of sugar
a pinch of salt

METHOD Start with the choux. Preheat the oven to 200°C/180°C fan/ gas mark 6. Grease 2 baking trays and line them with baking paper.

Put the water, sugar, butter and salt into a small non-stick saucepan on a medium heat. Take it off as soon as it comes to the boil and all the butter has melted. Add all the flour at once, stirring vigorously to avoid lumps.

Now step away for a few minutes to allow it to cool just slightly. Add the eggs a little at a time, making sure to stir continuously – it will look bitty and not smooth, but the more you mix, the more it will come together into a smooth paste. When the spoon is lifted the mixture should drop in a V-shape, and that's the perfect consistency.

Pop the mixture into a piping bag, or a zip-lock bag, and snip off the end, 2cm wide. Pipe small mounds on to the prepared baking sheets. Or you could just dollop teaspoons of the mixture on to them.

Wet your fingertips and pat down any peaks to prevent the choux burning in the oven. Bake for 25–30 minutes until light and crispy. Take out, cut in half horizontally, then put them back into the oven to dry a little more.

Meanwhile, make the pâté. Put the mackerel, yoghurt, butter, salt and pepper into a food processor and blitz to a smooth paste. If it is too stiff, add yoghurt a spoonful at a time until the mixture is smooth and glides effortlessly in the processor. Transfer to a serving bowl, cover and pop into the fridge.

Now make the pineapple chutney. Drain the pineapple chunks in a sieve and use the back of a spoon to squeeze out any extra moisture. Pop the chunks into a blender, along with the coriander, chillies, lime juice and zest. Blend to a smooth green paste. Have a taste – there should be a good balance of sweet and salty. Adjust by adding sugar or salt.

I like to put the crisp choux in the centre of the table, with the pâté and chutney, and let everyone make their own by sandwiching the choux halves with the pâté and adding a generous helping of chutney. But if I'm having people round I will assemble them all in advance.

SMOKED MACKEREL PÂTÉ CHOUX
with Green Pineapple Chutney

When I make ribs it's normally because we need our fix. It's rarely a meal or a sit-down event, simply something to get our teeth into. But you can easily turn them into a full meal if you serve other things alongside. I like using lamb ribs, which cook quickly rather than long and slow – thank god, because once I start thinking about these delicious ribs covered in sweet, sticky sauce, I want them to be ready to eat fast!

SERVES 4

PREP 20 MINS

COOK 1 HOUR
10 MINS

INGREDIENTS

1kg lamb ribs

10g soft light
brown sugar

2 tbsp honey

3 tbsp Worcestershire
sauce

3 tbsp balsamic vinegar

3 tbsp soy sauce

1 tsp ground ginger

1 tsp garlic powder

1 tsp ground coriander

1 tsp chilli flakes

For the garnish
2 large spring onions,
finely chopped

1 tbsp sesame seeds

a large handful of
fresh coriander,
roughly chopped

1 red chilli, finely sliced

METHOD Put the ribs into a large saucepan and cover with water. Bring to the boil on a high heat, then turn the heat down to medium until the ribs have cooked through. It takes about 45–50 minutes' simmering until they are tender. This will help reduce the cooking time in the oven and minimize some of the fat around the ribs. Skim off any foam that rises to the top of the water.

While the ribs are boiling, put the sugar and honey into a pan over a medium heat, giving it a stir occasionally. Once the sugar has melted and the caramel is a deep brown, take the pan off the heat. Stir in the Worcestershire sauce, balsamic and soy sauce, then add the ginger, garlic, coriander and chilli flakes. Stir well and set aside.

Preheat the oven to 220°C/200°C fan/gas mark 7. Have a roasting tray ready, lined with baking paper – this will help avoid having a monumental sticky mess to clear up afterwards.

Once the ribs are tender, take them out of the pan and drain them. Pop them into the roasting tray and put them into the oven for 10 minutes, then take them out again and brush the sticky glaze on top, making sure to cover every ribby crevice. Get ready to stare into the oven for another 10 minutes, basting them halfway through.

Mix the spring onions, sesame seeds, coriander and chilli in a bowl. As soon as those ribs are out, get them into a serving dish. We have all suffered burnt wrists from the lack of restraint. Sprinkle over the garnish and eat straight away.

LAMB RIBS

SERVES 4-6

PREP 25 MINS

COOK 15 MINS

To me, the test of any restaurant is whether they serve really good chips, be they chunky, fries, sweet potatoes, matchstick, or another variation. Whatever they are, they need to be good, and they are always the first things I look for on a menu. And now, I think life just got a tiny bit better, as this is a recipe not just for fries, but for fries made with cheese! They have a light, crisp, outer shell and the halloumi cheese goes all gooey and creamy as it warms up.

INGREDIENTS

4 x 250g blocks of halloumi cheese, each cut into 12 chips

150g plain flour

1½ tsp salt

3 tsp paprika

6 tsp garlic powder

2 eggs, beaten

1.5 litres vegetable oil, for frying

For the garnish

150ml soured cream

a large pinch of rock salt

1 tbsp za'atar

a large handful of fresh mint, roughly chopped

1 tsp chilli flakes

40g pomegranate seeds

METHOD Pat the cheese dry to remove any excess moisture.

Put the flour, salt, paprika and garlic on to a plate and mix till well combined. Place the beaten eggs in a dish alongside. Have a baking tray at the ready, large enough to lay all the chips on.

Coat the cheese first in the beaten egg, then in the flour, and pop on to the tray. Make sure you cover them evenly – though not to worry, they will get another layer very soon.

Once you have done all of them, take each floured bit of cheese and put it back into the flour for a second coating.

Put the oil into a medium saucepan on a high heat. If you have a thermometer, the temperature of the oil should be 150°C for a slow, gentle deep-fry. If you don't, to test whether the oil is hot enough, drop a breadcrumb in and if it floats, it's ready. Lower the heat and add a few bits of cheese to the pan – not too many, as they need to be able to move around. Be careful not to overcrowd the pan or this will reduce the temperature of the oil too much.

Have a baking tray at the ready and the oven set to 180°C/160°C fan/ gas mark 4.

The chips will take about 2–3 minutes. The outside should be deep golden brown. With a slotted spoon, take out the fries and put them on the baking tray. Put the tray into the oven to keep the cheese warm and the outside crisp. Fry the rest of the chips in batches, making sure to keep them warm in the oven as you go.

Once you are ready to serve, drizzle over the soured cream, sprinkle over the salt, za'atar, mint and chilli flakes, and top with the stunningly pink pomegranate seeds. Fries just got exotic!

CHUNKY HALLOUMI CHIPS

SERVES 4-6

PREP 20 MINS

NO COOK

Brussels sprouts don't always have to mean Christmas, and they certainly do not have to mean over-cooked vegetables! Something you might not know is that they are delicious raw and can be used just like cabbage is used in coleslaw. So this is my sprout slaw recipe, which is zesty, creamy and crunchy – all the things a slaw should be! Brussels sprouts are for life, not just for Christmas.

INGREDIENTS

250g trimmed
Brussels sprouts

1 red onion, thinly sliced

2 carrots, peeled
and grated

100g cashew nuts,
roughly chopped

1 tsp cumin seeds

100g Greek yoghurt

50g full-fat mayonnaise

1 tbsp wholegrain
mustard

½ a lemon, zest and juice

a large handful of fresh
chives, finely chopped

a large handful of fresh
flat-leaf parsley,
roughly chopped

METHOD I like using sprouts that are already trimmed – if I trim them myself I get stressed about waste. Even though the outer leaves are tough, I feel bad getting rid of them, so I go for ready-prepared.

I like to thinly slice the sprouts by hand, but if I'm rushed for time another really good way of doing it is in the food processor with a slicing blade.

Put the sprouts into a bowl with the onion, carrots, cashews and cumin seeds and mix well.

Put the yoghurt, mayonnaise, mustard, lemon juice and zest into a second, smaller bowl and mix really well. Add to the bowl of chopped vegetables, stirring it in and making sure that the creamy coating covers all the veg. If you like your slaw extra creamy, just add extra mayonnaise and yoghurt.

Add the chopped chives and parsley and mix in well.

And if anyone says they don't like sprouts, give them this slaw instead and ask the question again.

BRUSSELS SPROUT SLAW

I ate these unique fries at a chain restaurant with my family recently. We all tried them and immediately stared at one another, eyes rolling back into our heads. My son said, 'Ma, you *need* to make these!' It was my sentiment exactly. The matchstick fries are beautifully crisp, but it's their sweet fishy coating that is the real star, sprinkled with a nutty, garlicky, seaweedy deliciousness. I have tried my best to create the same wonderful outcome, so we can all have them together at home and it won't cost close to a fiver for a few mouthfuls.

SERVES 4-6

PREP 25 MINS

COOK 20 MINS

INGREDIENTS

For the seasoning mix
2 nori sheets
6 tbsp garlic granules
2 tsp chilli flakes
3 tbsp white sesame seeds
1 tbsp black sesame seeds

For the fries
1kg potatoes
(large baking potatoes are
usually best)
1.5 litres vegetable oil,
for frying

For the sticky sauce
2 tbsp honey
1 tbsp fish sauce
1 tbsp oyster sauce

METHOD Start by making the seasoning mix. Put the nori sheets, garlic and chilli flakes into a food processor and blitz until the nori has broken up. Transfer into a bowl and add the white and black sesame seeds. Mix and set aside.

To make the fries, thinly slice the potatoes, then cut them into thin matchsticks. Put them into a bowl of water. Have a damp towel at the ready to wrap the fries and stop them browning when you take them out.

Put a large saucepan on a high heat and add the oil. When the oil is hot, drop in a piece of potato and if it rises to the top, the oil is ready for frying.

Heat the oven to 180°C/160°C fan/gas mark 4 to keep the fries warm. Have 2 baking trays ready, lined with kitchen paper.

Dry the matchstick potatoes in the towel, then put a large handful into the oil. Don't overcrowd the pan – fry them in batches. Once the fries are golden brown they are ready – this should take about 3 minutes. Take them out with a slotted spoon, put them on the prepared tray, and place them in the oven to keep warm.

Once all the chips have been fried, transfer them to a serving dish.

Mix together the honey, fish sauce and oyster sauce. Drizzle all over the chips and toss to make sure they are all lightly coated. Sprinkle generously with the seasoning mix, and serve while still warm.

SERVES 4

PREP 20 MINS

COOK 25 MINS

American food trends fascinate me, and the blooming onion is something I've seen popping up everywhere on social media, from US food writers and on cooking blogs. Here I have created something very similar, but rather than deep-frying the whole onion I have opted for a healthier, less oily version. (Nothing wrong with a deep-fry, but sometimes, *just sometimes*, it's good to have options.) These beautiful crisp onions 'bloom' as they bake, creating a little space in the centre for a dollop of dip.

INGREDIENTS

For the onions

2 large Spanish onions

2 egg whites

70g fine natural breadcrumbs

30g plain flour

1 tsp salt

2 tsp cayenne pepper

spray oil

For the sriracha mayo dip

100g full-fat mayonnaise

3 tbsp sriracha

METHOD Preheat the oven to 200°C/180°C fan/ gas mark 6.

To prepare the onions, peel them from the root (make very sure not to peel from the tip!). Try to avoid taking too much of the root itself away as it helps the onions to stay intact.

Place one of the onions on a work surface, sitting on its root. Using a sharp knife, cut down the centre but stop when you get a centimetre away from the base – you don't want to go all the way through.

Now turn the onion and do the same again, creating a cross, but making sure not to go all the way down. For each quartered section, cut down again from the centre point to create another two triangles.

Do the exact same thing to the other onion. Now tease the onions to encourage them to open. Put them on a baking tray.

Put the egg whites into a bowl and whisk until they are just light and fluffy. This should only take a few minutes.

Put the breadcrumbs, flour, salt and cayenne into a bowl (big enough to fit one onion in at a time). Mix together.

Brush one of the onions all over with the egg white, being sure to get into all the corners and in between all the onion layers. Once you are confident that the onion is covered, dip it gently into the breadcrumb mix. Pop it back on the baking tray and do the same to the other onion. Now scatter the remaining breadcrumb mix in and over both onions. Spray the onions with a good mist of oil.

Cover with foil and bake in the preheated oven for 15 minutes, then take the foil off and bake uncovered for another 10 minutes.

To make the dip, mix together the mayo and sriracha.

Take the onions out of the oven and serve with pots of the dip.

CRISPY BLOOMING ONIONS

SERVES 6

PREP 20 MINS

COOK 20 MINS

My mum used to make tempura using leftover peelings and old veg. Like her, I am not very good at wasting, but thank goodness I have discovered composting, otherwise I would eat everything in sight, edible or not! For this delicious recipe, thinly sliced courgettes are lightly coated in a Parmesan tempura batter and fried – they are great as a side or as something extra to go alongside a meal. I like to eat them with steak instead of (or sometimes as well as) chips.

INGREDIENTS

4 small courgettes (about 500g), thinly sliced at a slant

500ml vegetable oil, for frying

75g plain flour, plus 2 tbsp for dusting

75g cornflour

a large pinch of salt

2 medium egg whites

150g Parmesan cheese, finely grated

1 lemon, zest only

200ml sparkling water

salt

Parmesan shavings, to serve

METHOD Put the sliced courgettes into a bowl and dust them with the 2 tablespoons of flour. Toss them around in the bowl, making sure each one is coated well.

Put the oil into a medium saucepan on a high heat.

To make the batter, put the plain flour and cornflour into a bowl with a pinch of salt and whisk together. Add the egg whites, Parmesan and lemon zest and whisk well. The batter should be thick at this point. Add half the sparkling water and whisk to get rid of any lumps, then add the rest of the water and whisk until well combined.

Test the oil by dropping in a little of the batter. If it rises to the surface the oil is ready. Lower the heat to medium.

Gently drop slices of courgette into the oil, one at a time. Fry them in batches, making sure not to overcrowd the pan. Have a tray with kitchen paper at the ready, to drain off excess oil. They only take 4–5 minutes to fry. Make sure you keep turning them and moving them around.

As soon as the courgettes come out of the pan, sprinkle them with salt. Fry the rest of the courgette slices the same way, sprinkling them with salt each time. Serve sprinkled with the Parmesan shavings.

COURGETTE PARMESAN TEMPURA

Dinner

When I've had a super-long day – doing whatever I'm busy doing – I find that the need to sit down, eat and talk about the day with my family becomes more important than ever. Everything I do feels full-time at the moment: full-time cook, full-time writer, full-time mum, wife, insomniac, complainer, bore, etc.! Some days a whole 12 hours go by and I get home to realize I haven't eaten a thing. That makes dinner all the more crucial. Just to have a few hours in the evening catching up with my family is the recuperation I need. I love to get into the kitchen and cook from my heart, whether it's a Pot Pizza, Chilli with Cornbread or Prawn Biryani. Some weeks are so busy we put dinner in the diary. If it's in the diary, then I know I have to get back in time, and they know to wait for me. Dinner, to me, means I'm home.

I grew up using my fingers to eat, which was the traditional way in our home. Though I have since mastered a bit of cutlery, I still find there is something really rather satisfying about eating with your hands. I think food tastes better when it is not obstructed by a foreign object between you and that delicious mouthful. Anyway, I applaud anyone who can successfully use cutlery to eat these crisp shell tacos. They're filled with Bombay potatoes and served with delicious paprika and cheese corn-on-the-cobs on the side.

SERVES 4

PREP 25 MINS

COOK 50 MINS

INGREDIENTS

4 small flour tortillas (wholemeal if you prefer)

lettuce, sliced, to serve

Bombay mix, to serve

For the Bombay potatoes

4 tbsp olive oil

1 clove of garlic, chopped

1 red onion, cut into large chunks

1 tsp salt

1 tsp tomato purée

10 cherry tomatoes

¼ tsp ground turmeric

1 tsp onion seeds

1 orange pepper, cut into chunks

500g potatoes, peeled and cut into chunks

2 large carrots, cut into coins and the coins halved

150ml water

2 tsp tamarind paste

a large handful of fresh coriander

METHOD Start by making the Bombay potatoes. Put a large non-stick frying pan or wok on a high heat. Put the oil into the pan and, as soon as it is hot, add the garlic. It will cook fast, so be ready. As soon as the garlic is brown, add the onion and salt and cook for just 5 minutes. My memory of Bombay potatoes at my dad's restaurant was that the veg was always very visible. So, less cooking is key.

Add the tomato purée, then add the cherry tomatoes one by one, piercing each tomato as you go along – this will allow the steam to come out as they cook, so we can prevent an almighty tomato explosion (I still have a tomato stain that needs clearing up). Stir and allow the tomatoes to soften just slightly.

Add the turmeric and onion seeds and cook for just a few minutes, then add the orange pepper, potatoes and carrots. Stir, then add the water, which will just allow the potatoes and carrots to steam. Pop a lid on the pan and cook for 25 minutes on a low to medium heat.

Take off the lid, then stir and leave to cook with the lid off for 10 minutes to dry out the mixture. You will know it is ready when the potatoes, if pierced, don't resist, and the carrots are still slightly firm. Give everything an occasional stir just to make sure nothing is sticking and adjust the heat if necessary. All our cookers are different, so just keep an eye.

While the potatoes are cooking, start the corn. Place the cobs in a pan of boiling water and boil for 10 minutes. Put a griddle pan on a high heat.

Once the potatoes are ready, take them off the heat and stir in the tamarind paste and coriander. Leave the lid on to keep them warm while you make the tacos and corn.

→|

BOMBAY POTATO TACOS
with Paprika Corn-on-the-cobs

For the corn-on-the-cob

4 full-size corn cobs

100g full-fat
mayonnaise

1 tsp paprika

salt

50g Cheddar cheese,
finely grated

When the corn cobs have been boiling for 10 minutes, take them straight out of the pan and on to the hot griddle to get charred. The best way to get really good charring is to put the corn down following the lines of the griddle. Keep moving them around and turning, so that they can char all over. This can take 10–15 minutes.

Take the cobs off the griddle and place them on a board or plate. Smother each cob with mayonnaise – be generous! Sprinkle with paprika and salt, making sure to roll each cob so it gets covered all over. Sprinkle with the cheese.

Whack the oven on to 200°C/180°C fan/gas mark 6. Take any trays out of the oven and just pull out the slatted shelves enough so you can assemble the tacos in the gaps – that balancing act where the shelf will stay put and not fall on the floor. Slot a tortilla through one of the slats, then, leaving a gap of 2 or maybe 3 slats, slide the other half through. Just like hanging huge sheets on banisters. Do the same with the other 3 tortillas. Keep them close together – this will stop them opening up too wide.

The tortillas should take around 6 minutes. The first time I made these I took my eye off them, so I highly recommend a timer if you're easily distracted like me.

Keep checking the tortillas as they cook. They are done when they form that distinct hard-shell shape. Take them out and set aside.

Make your taco by filling each shell with Bombay potatoes, sliced lettuce and Bombay mix and serve the paprika corn-on-the-cobs alongside. I like a lettuce/potatoes/lettuce/potatoes pattern, topped with a shower of Bombay mix. Word of warning: it's about to get messy.

INGREDIENTS

For the chilli

3 tbsp olive oil

3 cloves of garlic, chopped

1 stick of cinnamon

1kg beef mince

1 tsp yeast extract
(Marmite, Vegemite, etc.)

2 tsp salt

3 tbsp tomato purée

1 tbsp ground cumin

1 tbsp ground coriander

250ml red grape juice

1 x 400g tin of chopped
tomatoes

2 x 400g tins of kidney
beans, drained

a large handful of fresh
coriander, chopped

For the jalapeño cornbread

375g plain flour

225g cornmeal

1 tsp salt

4 tsp baking powder

110g caster sugar

480ml whole milk

2 medium eggs,
lightly beaten

110g unsalted butter,
melted, plus extra
for greasing

215g jar of sliced green
jalapeños, drained

100g Cheddar cheese,
grated

Chilli is the saviour of dinner times when you have anyone under the age of 18 to feed. It freezes well, and feeds generously. This chilli is cooked long and slow, with grape juice for extra sweetness. It is warm, satisfying and so versatile, as it can be eaten with baked potatoes, rice, pasta, in a wrap, or – my favourite – with this jalapeño cornbread.

SERVES 6   PREP 25 MINS   COOK 1 HOUR 20 MINS

METHOD For the chilli, put a large saucepan on the hob on a high heat. Add the oil and once it is hot add the garlic and cinnamon. As soon as the garlic is brown, add the beef mince and cook until browned all over. If there is a lot of fat in the pan after the mince has cooked, spoon some out.

Add the yeast extract, salt and tomato purée. If you are not a fan of the old yeast extract, I assure you it's not that bad – it gives the chilli a richer flavour, and you won't be able to tell it's there.

Cook for a few minutes, then stir in the ground cumin and coriander and cook for about 5 minutes more.

Add the grape juice and tinned tomatoes and stir, then add the drained kidney beans. Pop a lid on the pan and leave to cook on a medium heat for at least 1 hour. Stir occasionally to check whether it's catching on the base. If it is, just turn the heat down.

Now for the cornbread. Preheat the oven to 200°C/180°C fan/ gas mark 6. Grease the base of a 23cm square cake tin and line with baking paper.

Put the flour, cornmeal, salt, baking powder and sugar into a large mixing bowl and stir to combine. Make a well in the centre and add the milk, beaten eggs and melted butter. Using a hand-held mixer, beat the mixture until it has a cake batter-type consistency.

Pour into the prepared tin and level the surface. Spread over the jalapeños and sprinkle over the grated cheese. Bake in the oven for 40–45 minutes.

Leave to cool in the tin for 10 minutes, then take out and cut into squares. Stir the coriander into the chilli and rootle through to take out the cinnamon stick. Be sure to get rid of that! Now you are good to go.

BEEF CHILLI with Jalapeño Cornbread

As a family we try hard to avoid meat and fish during the week. This gives our digestive systems a little break and allows me to think out of the box when I'm cooking. It's all too easy to whack on a curry or put some fish fingers in the oven. Nothing wrong with that of course, but when I know we are eating well, I can sleep better at night! Being often rushed for time, I found this amazing way to create a sauce that doesn't need cooking, just blitzing. The creamy avocado works so well with the fresh mint and peas. It's green and it's good!

SERVES 4

PREP 15 MINS

COOK 10 MINS

INGREDIENTS

375g pasta

1 large avocado
(or 2 small)

2 cloves of garlic

2 tbsp coconut oil,
melted

½ tsp salt

1 lemon, juice and zest

6 fresh mint leaves

150g fresh peas (or
frozen and defrosted)

1 large frozen red chilli
(optional)

METHOD Cook the pasta according to the instructions on the packet. Once it is cooked and drained, set it aside.

This next step is by far the easiest bit. Think of the washing-up, or the lack of it! De-stone the avocado, then put the avocado flesh, garlic, coconut oil, salt, lemon juice, zest and mint leaves into a blender or smoothie-maker with 4 tablespoons of water. (Or you can even do this bit in a bowl or pan with a stick blender.)

Blend until you get a smooth paste. If you find the mixture is struggling to move, add another tablespoon of water and try again. Put the pasta into a serving bowl and pour over the sauce. Add the peas and mix until all the pasta is coated in green goodness.

For a little kick, I like to take a red chilli from the bag I always have in the freezer and just grate a tiny bit on top. This is optional, but worth doing if you like chilli.

AVOCADO PASTA
with Peas and Mint

BUTTER TURKEY

I always hear people complaining that turkey is dry, and in all fairness it often can be, especially the day after it's cooked. Despite being raised on curry, my solution isn't always to turn it into one, but on some occasions it really is the only answer. I love turkey because it's lean and takes on flavour well, so here I've created a twist on classic butter chicken by turning it into butter turkey. It's a delicious creamy curry that works so well with simple white rice. I'm not saying turkey should always be curried, but when it comes to the bits left over after Christmas dinner, this is a real step up from putting them into a sandwich.

SERVES 6

PREP 20 MINS

COOK 1 HOUR
15 MINS

INGREDIENTS

100g unsalted butter

1 whole bulb of garlic,
cloves separated
and peeled

60g fresh ginger, peeled

3 medium onions,
quartered

2 tsp salt

3 tbsp tomato purée

1kg turkey breast,
chopped into chunks

2 tbsp garam masala

2 tsp paprika

300ml water

100g salted cashews

To serve

natural yoghurt

a large handful of
fresh coriander,
roughly chopped

cooked white rice

METHOD Put a large saucepan on a high heat and add the butter. Let it melt completely.

Put the garlic and ginger into a food processor and blitz to a smooth paste. Add the paste to the hot butter and cook for about 5 minutes, until it has browned, being careful not to burn it.

Add the onions to the food processor and blitz until they are just chopped, not a paste. Pop them into the pan along with the salt and tomato purée, and cook for about 15 minutes, until the onions are really soft.

Add the chopped turkey and cook for about 10 minutes with the lid off.

Add the garam masala and paprika and cook for 10 minutes, stirring occasionally.

Add the water, stir and pop the lid on. Cook for 15 minutes, then take the lid off. Add the cashews and cook for another 10 minutes.

Serve drizzled with yoghurt and sprinkled with chopped coriander, along-side plenty of hot, fluffy rice.

SEAFOOD CRUMBLE

This recipe takes inspiration from – you guessed right – an apple crumble. I promise there are no apples in here, but there is a crumble top! This is a simple fish pie of the kind my kids love, but with an oaty, buttery cayenne topping. When I first served it to the children, I told them it was a crumble but kept quiet about the fish bit, and they all got a big surprise when they took a bite. Luckily, the initial shock soon turned to happiness.

SERVES 4

PREP 20 MINS

COOK 45 MINS

INGREDIENTS

For the filling
3 large eggs
400ml whole milk
400g frozen fish pie mix, defrosted
25g unsalted butter
25g plain flour
1 tsp mustard powder
½ tsp salt
a handful of fresh chives, finely chopped
100g frozen peas

For the crumble
225g plain flour
150g unsalted butter
130g porridge oats
½ tsp salt
1 tsp cayenne pepper
75g crispy fried onions

To serve
garlic bread
green salad

METHOD Preheat the oven to 200°C/180°C fan/gas mark 6. Have a 20 x 30cm rectangular casserole dish at the ready.

Lower the eggs gently into boiling water and simmer for 8 minutes. Rinse under cold water and, when cool to touch, peel from their shells. Cut the eggs into quarters, and set aside.

Put the milk and fish into a small pan and warm gently till the fish is poached – this can take 3–4 minutes. Remove the fish from the pan to a plate, and set the milk aside.

Melt the butter in a medium pan. When it has melted, add the flour and stir it in well. Add the milk gradually, whisking all the time until it has all been poured in. Keep whisking until the mixture thickens. You will know it is ready when the mixture coats the back of a spoon.

Put the fish back into the sauce and add the mustard, salt, chives, peas and quartered eggs. Gently mix together, making sure not to break the fish up too much.

Pour the mixture into the casserole dish and start making the crumble. Put the flour and butter into a bowl. Rub the butter into the flour, then add the oats, salt, cayenne and crispy onions and mix it all together.

Scatter the crumble over the fish and bake in the oven for 25 minutes. We like to eat this with cheesy garlic bread and a green salad. Isn't that how all crumbles are eaten? Custard may have been a step too far!

I learnt to cook with cucumber from my mum and she learnt from her mum. When they first came over to this country, they missed the seasonal vegetables they were used to plucking off the vines in their village. They missed the comfort of home, so they had to find alternatives. The cucumber was a replacement for water bottle gourd, which looks totally different to cucumber but is very similar when cooked. It's this ingenuity that I love about people who miss home but make do with what they have. Of course, my mum can now buy all the vegetables that she couldn't in the 70s, but I quite like the cucumber so I'm keeping it for myself. I love it in a broth with fish. Simple and delicious.

SERVES **4**

PREP **15 MINS**

COOK **1 HOUR**

INGREDIENTS

260g skinless cod fillets, chopped into 3cm cubes

1 tsp ground turmeric

5 tbsp olive oil

3 cloves of garlic, chopped

1 small onion, finely chopped

1 tsp salt

1 tsp chilli powder

1 tsp ground cumin

1 large cucumber, topped and tailed, cut into 1cm coins and each coin halved (about 600g)

750ml fish stock (or water)

1 lemon, juice only

a large handful of fresh coriander, roughly chopped

2 spring onions, finely sliced

METHOD Put a large non-stick saucepan on a high heat. Put the fish cubes into a small bowl with ½ teaspoon of turmeric and 3 tablespoons of the oil. Mix until the pieces of fish are coated, then put them into the pan and fry until they are sealed with a nice crust. The fish should only take a few minutes to cook on each side. Remove from the pan and set aside.

Add the rest of the oil to the pan along with the garlic and cook until it is golden brown – this should take about 5 minutes. Add the onion and salt and cook until the onion is tender and almost mushy, this can take about 15 minutes.

Add the chilli powder, cumin and the remaining ½ teaspoon of turmeric. Mix through just for a minute, then add all the cucumber. Stir to coat the cucumber in the spices, then pour in the fish stock. Put a lid on the pan and cook the broth for 30 minutes.

After 30 minutes, pierce the cucumber with a knife – it should be nice and tender. You will know when it's ready, as it should look translucent.

Add the fish and warm it through. If you find the liquid has been absorbed and it needs more, add a little extra water. Once the fish has warmed through, take the pan off the heat. Add the lemon juice, coriander and spring onions, stir, and it is ready to serve. This is just the kind of thing I would eat when I've had a breakfast- and lunch-heavy day and I only want a light dinner.

CUCUMBER AND COD BROTH

PRAWN SAFFRON BIRYANI

I'd never made a biryani until my sister married her Punjabi husband. She learnt all sorts of tips and tricks, which she passed my way. As soon as I'd mastered the basics, I couldn't resist venturing off into new and exciting combinations. This prawn saffron biryani is a lighter and zestier version of its meatier counterpart. I love the idea that an entire meal is made in one pot. It's not all about the flavour; it's also about the lack of washing-up! Indian five-spice is made up of cumin seeds, brown mustard seeds, fennel seeds, fenugreek and nigella seeds. If you can't find it as a mix, you can buy the spices separately, mix them together in equal amounts and store in a jar.

SERVES 4

PREP 15 MINS

COOK 50 MINS

INGREDIENTS

500g basmati rice

1.5 litres cold water

a large pinch of saffron

1 small cinnamon stick

2 tsp salt

For the sauce

80g unsalted butter

5 cloves of garlic, chopped

2 medium onions, chopped

2 tsp salt

½ a lemon

2 large red chillies, quartered

½ tsp ground turmeric

1 tsp Indian five-spice (see intro)

a large handful of fresh parsley, chopped

350g raw king prawns, shelled

5 tbsp olive oil

METHOD Put the rice into a large saucepan with the water, saffron, cinnamon and salt. Place on a high heat and boil for 8 minutes, stirring occasionally to stop the rice sticking to the base. Drain through a sieve and set aside.

To make the sauce, put the same saucepan back on the hob and turn the heat up to high. Add the butter, then, as soon as the butter is hot, add the garlic and let it brown for about 4–5 minutes. Add the onions and salt and cook until the onions are soft – this can take 15 minutes.

Squeeze in the juice of the half lemon, then cut the lemon rind into thin slices and add to the pan.

Add the chillies, turmeric and five-spice, and stir for 5 minutes to cook the spices. Take off the heat and add the parsley and prawns. Stir well, so the prawns are coated. The prawns don't need cooking in the sauce – they will steam and cook in the biryani (otherwise they run the risk of becoming dry and rubbery).

Take a large pan, something you would be happy to serve up in, and pour the oil into the base. Swirl it around so some of the oil goes up the sides.

Pop in half the rice and spread it evenly across the bottom of the pan. Put all the prawn mixture on top of the rice.

Put the rest of the rice on top of the prawns. Put the lid on firmly and place on a high heat for 5 minutes, then turn the heat down completely. Leave to cook for 20 minutes, then serve.

PUFFED-RICE HADDOCK
with Chips and Curry Sauce

Haddock and chips – need I say more? We love buying a large portion from the takeaway and sharing it straight out of the bag, getting a cheeky fix without eating a whole plateful each. But I also love cooking my own version at home, making things a bit healthier by coating the haddock in a crust of puffed rice, rather than greasy batter. Served with chips and homemade curry sauce, this is our favourite on date nights.

SERVES 2

PREP 20 MINS

COOK 35 MINS

INGREDIENTS

For the curry sauce
25g unsalted butter
1 small onion, chopped
1 tsp chilli flakes
½ tsp salt
½ lemon, juice only
1 tbsp curry powder
1 tsp plain flour
100ml vegetable stock
100ml double cream

For the chips
4 tbsp olive oil
200g frozen chips
salt

For the haddock
2 tbsp olive oil
2 pieces of haddock (220g)
1 tsp salt
1 tsp paprika
1 egg, beaten
40g rice puffs, crushed
peas, to serve

METHOD Start by making the sauce. Put a small pan on a medium heat. Put in the butter and let it melt. Add the onion, chilli flakes and salt and cook until the onion is tender – about 10–15 minutes. Add the lemon juice, curry powder and plain flour. The mixture will be dry.

Add the stock and boil for about 2 minutes, allowing the flour to cook out. Blitz, using a hand blender, until the mixture is smooth. Stir in the cream, then cover the pan and set aside to keep warm.

Put a non-stick frying pan on the hob on a high heat and add the oil. Throw in the frozen chips and fry them from frozen until they are crisp. Be sure to toss them around and stir. They will take about 15 minutes. Once they are cooked, take them out of the pan and sprinkle with salt.

To cook the haddock, add another 2 tablespoons of oil to the pan. Dust the fish with salt and paprika, making sure to cover it all over. Dip first in the beaten egg and then in the crushed cereal. Pat the crust all over.

Drop the fish gently into the oil and cook on one side for 5 minutes, then flip over and fry for about 2–3 minutes on the other side.

Serve the fish hot, with the chips and curry sauce on top. We always have some boiled frozen peas on the side.

SERVES 5

PREP 20 MINS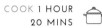

COOK 1 HOUR
20 MINS

For me, burgers are the stuff of dreams. When I cook my own I never make the same type twice. And this particular burger is extra special: a meaty beef patty, melted smoked cheese and a runny egg, all welded together with a sticky, smoky bacon jam, then topped and tailed with a sweet brioche bun. Surely that is what a burger is all about, getting everything in one mouthful? It's all too easy to buy burgers, but my goodness it's worth making them at least once in your life!

INGREDIENTS

For the bacon jam

3 tbsp olive oil

3 cloves of garlic, chopped

1 small onion, finely diced

1 tsp chilli flakes

450g halal bacon or streaky bacon, thinly sliced

1 tbsp instant coffee

125ml hot water

40g soft brown sugar

60ml malt vinegar

85ml maple syrup

For the beef burgers

1kg beef mince

1 tsp onion salt

1 tsp freshly ground black pepper

1 tsp garlic granules

2 tbsp sunflower oil, for frying

Everything else you need for the burger

5 slices of smoked cheese

5 large brioche buns

5 lettuce leaves

extra oil, for frying

5 large eggs

METHOD Begin by making the jam. Put a medium saucepan on a medium heat. Add the oil and as soon the oil is hot, add the garlic, onion and chilli flakes. Cook until the onion is tender.

Add the bacon and cook for a few minutes.

Stir the instant coffee into the hot water along with the sugar. Add to the bacon and onion. Now add the vinegar and maple syrup and turn the heat to high. Once it boils, turn the heat down and leave to cook gently on a low to medium heat for at least an hour, until all the liquid has reduced and it takes on a sticky jam texture.

I like to leave the jam bitty, but if you prefer it smooth you can blitz it in a blender. Set aside.

Now make the simple burgers. Put the beef mince into a bowl and add the onion salt, pepper and garlic. Get your hands in there and mix until everything is well combined. Divide the mixture into 5 equal amounts, about 200g each. Squash them into patties, making sure they are not thick in the centre.

Place a large non-stick frying pan on a high heat. Add the oil, then gently place the patties in the pan. Fry for 5 minutes on one side, then flip them over and fry for 5 minutes on the other side. Place a slice of the cheese on each patty and just give it a few minutes to melt. Once the patties are cooked, put them on a tray.

Split your brioche buns and toast both sides. Once they are toasted, place a lettuce leaf and a patty on one half of the brioche, cheese side up, and smother the bacon jam over the top. Using the same pan, add a little extra oil and whack the heat up. Fry the eggs until crispy around the edges – I like to keep my yolk runny, but if you don't, cook until the yolks are firm.

Lay a fried egg on top of each cheese-topped patty. Put the other half of the brioche on top, and enjoy.

BEEF BURGERS
with Bacon Jam

FREE-FORM SAUSAGES
with Broccoli Mash and Red Onion Gravy

INGREDIENTS

For the sausages

900g lamb mince

1½ tsp salt

2 tsp garlic granules

3 tsp onion granules

1½ tsp mustard powder

1 tsp paprika

4 tsp dried parsley

50g fine dried
breadcrumbs

oil, for greasing tray
and hands

*For the onion gravy
(makes 600ml)*

50g unsalted butter

3 medium onions,
thinly sliced

½ tsp salt

2 tbsp Worcestershire
sauce

2 tsp mustard powder

1 tbsp plain flour

500ml chicken stock or
hot water

For the broccoli mash

2 heads of broccoli,
florets only, main
stem removed

4 tbsp full-fat cream
cheese

a pinch of salt

1 tsp freshly ground
black pepper

I prefer not to eat the same old things over and over, so I'm always looking for ways to rethink our favourite meals. Such as this, my alternative version of bangers and mash with onion gravy. It's essentially a recipe for homemade sausages, but with no need to put the meat into a skin (which my husband is very happy about, since he really hates the skins!). They're served up with creamy broccoli mash and a simple onion gravy.

SERVES 4   PREP 30 MINS   COOK 30 MINS

METHOD Preheat the oven to 200°C/180°C fan/gas mark 6. Lightly grease the base of a baking tray with sides.

To make the sausages, put the mince, salt, garlic, onion, mustard, paprika, parsley and breadcrumbs into a bowl. Using your hands, give it a really good mix so everything is well combined. Divide into 8 mounds.

Wash your hands and smother them with oil. Shape each mound into a sausage shape (these are not for the faint-hearted and are meant to fill you up!). Place them on the baking tray, then pop them into the oven and bake for 30 minutes. Meanwhile, you can prepare everything else.

Start on the onion gravy by putting a medium saucepan on a high heat. Add the butter and, as soon as it has melted, add the onions, salt, Worcestershire sauce and mustard. Cook until the onions are soft, tender and, as my kids like to describe them, droopy!

Once the onions have softened, stir in the flour. Cook for a few minutes, then pour in the stock. Cook on a high heat until the mixture has thickened – this should take about 10 minutes.

Meanwhile, to make the mash, put the florets into a microwave-safe bowl. Add a splash of water and cover with clingfilm. Microwave on high for 8 minutes, or until the broccoli is very tender.

Put the broccoli into a blender with the cream cheese, salt and pepper and blend to a smooth, mash-like consistency.

By now the sausages should be ready. Take them out of the oven and serve with the broccoli mash and the warm onion gravy.

JOLLOF PILAU
with Salted Cucumber Salad

African street food is becoming very popular and I love the flavours of jollof rice, which in some ways tastes similar to the food I grew up eating, and in others is entirely different. Jollof rice is also my brother's favourite, so I've created an easy recipe for him to use at home. This simple pilau is cooked in one pot and has all the distinctive jollof flavours. For a protein hit, I add vegetarian chicken-style pieces, which soak up all the spices.

SERVES 4-5

PREP 40 MINS

COOK 30 MINS

INGREDIENTS

For the jollof spice mix
30g ground ginger
30g garlic powder
45g chilli flakes
20g dried thyme
20g ground cinnamon
15g ground nutmeg
20g dried coriander
1 tbsp salt
1 tbsp ground black pepper

For the salted cucumber
1 large cucumber, halved lengthways, thinly sliced
1 red onion, thinly sliced
20g rock salt

For the pilau
500g basmati rice
5 tbsp olive oil
1 medium onion, diced
2 tsp salt
300g vegetarian chicken-style pieces
4 tbsp jollof spice mix (see above)

METHOD Start by making the jollof spice mix. Put all the spices into a large jar. We only need a little for this recipe – the rest can be safely put away for another occasion.

Soak the rice in cold water.

Make the salted cucumber by putting the cucumber, onion and salt into a bowl. Give it a stir and set aside.

To make the pilau, you need a large saucepan with a lid – the dish will be made in one pot. Put the pan on a high heat and add the oil. As soon as the oil is hot, add the onion and salt, and cook until the onion is soft.

Now add the chicken-style pieces and fry them with the onion for a few minutes. Add 4 tablespoons of the jollof spice mix and stir well. If the spices start to stick to the base of the pan, add a small splash of water. Cook the spices for at least 10 minutes on a low heat.

Drain the rice in a sieve, making sure you remove all the water. Add the rice to the pan of onion and chicken-style pieces, and stir it in so it gets coated with all the delicious spices.

Boil a full kettle of water and have it at the ready. Pour boiling water on to the rice and keep going until the water is a couple of centimetres above the rice. I like to be accurate, and I even have a rice ruler to make sure.

Boil on a high heat, making sure to stir all the time. As soon as all the water has been absorbed, pop a lid on the pan and leave the rice to steam for 15 minutes on the lowest hob setting. When the rice is ready, fluff it up, using a fork.

Drain the cucumber in a colander and rinse with a little water to get rid of excess salt. The cucumber and onion should be soft. Serve alongside the rice.

When I see fruit, I don't just see dessert or sweets. I love using fruit in my savoury cooking too. That's all thanks to my Bangladeshi home that I grew up in as a child. Citrus works just as well with savoury dishes as it does with sweet. The old grapefruit doesn't get much airtime though. I love its combination of sweet and bitter, which works really nicely with the chicken. This stew is such a simple thing to make, but the grapefruit adds some razzle dazzle.

SERVES 6

PREP 20 MINS

COOK 1 HOUR

INGREDIENTS

For the stew

1kg skinless boneless chicken thighs, diced

1 tsp ground turmeric

4 tbsp olive oil, plus a little extra

3 cloves of garlic, chopped

1 small onion, finely diced

1 tsp salt

2 tsp ground cumin

1 tsp chilli flakes

1 large grapefruit, juice (about 150ml) and zest

500ml hot water

2 tbsp cornflour mixed with 2 tbsp water

a large handful of fresh flat-leaf parsley, finely chopped

For the couscous

400g couscous

1 tsp salt

2 tbsp unsalted butter (30g)

550ml boiling water

METHOD Put the chicken into a bowl, add ½ teaspoon of turmeric and mix until all the chicken is covered. Place a large saucepan on the hob on a medium to high heat and add the oil. Fry the chicken in batches, until cooked and brown around the edges. Put back into the bowl and set aside.

Add a little extra oil, about a tablespoon, to the pan. Add the garlic, onion and salt and cook until the onion is soft – this can take 10–15 minutes.

Now add the cumin, chilli flakes and the remaining ½ teaspoon of turmeric and cook for a few minutes.

Add the grapefruit juice and zest, along with the browned chicken. Mix through, then add the hot water.

Stir in the cornflour/water mixture, then cover the pan with a lid and cook for 30 minutes.

Meanwhile, put the couscous into a bowl and stir in the salt. Put the butter on top. Pour in the boiling water until it reaches about 1cm above the couscous. Cover, then set aside so that the couscous can soak up the water.

When the chicken stew is cooked, take it off the heat and add the parsley. Serve the stew with the couscous.

GRAPEFRUIT CHICKEN STEW
with Couscous

FISH FINGER LASAGNE

I'm well aware you might be judging me right now! And my question to you is, how many fish fingers can you eat in one sitting? My record is eighteen. I'm sure it could be more, but eating more than eighteen fish fingers at once would just be plain greedy! Meanwhile, I have cooked fish fingers every which way, and one of our favourites is this fish finger lasagne. It's simple and creamy and is spiked with the addition of fresh tarragon.

SERVES 6

PREP 25 MINS

COOK 1 HOUR
10 MINS

INGREDIENTS

For the white sauce
1 litre whole milk

6 cloves of garlic, grated

40g unsalted butter

50g plain flour

1 tsp English mustard

1 tsp salt

For the fish finger filling
2 tbsp unsalted butter

1 large leek, finely chopped

½ tsp salt

2 tbsp fresh tarragon, finely chopped (or use dried)

20 fish fingers (about 500g), defrosted and chopped roughly into small chunks

12 lasagne sheets

200g Cheddar cheese, grated

METHOD Preheat the oven to 200°C/180°C fan/gas mark 6 and have a 20 x 30cm casserole dish ready.

To make the sauce, put the milk into a pan with the grated garlic. Bring it just to the boil, then take it off the heat.

Put another medium pan on a medium heat and add the butter. Let it melt, then add the flour and stir it into the butter until it forms a thick dough. Slowly ladle in the hot milk a little at a time, whisking until it's all been added. Keep whisking – the mixture should get thicker. Keep going until you have used up all the milk and the mixture coats the back of a spoon.

Take off the heat, stir in the mustard and salt, then set aside. As it cools the mixture will become thicker.

Now for the filling. Put a frying pan on a medium heat. Add the butter, and when it has melted add the leek and salt. Cook for about 15 minutes, until the leek has wilted and really softened.

Add the tarragon and the fish finger pieces and stir through. Cook for 10–15 minutes, breaking up the fish fingers slightly. Take off the heat.

Now to start layering. Spread a few spoonfuls of the white sauce evenly over the base of your casserole dish. Cover with 4 lasagne sheets. You may have to break the fourth piece to make it fit all the way to the edges.

Lay half the fish mixture on top of the lasagne sheets. Spread a third of the remaining white sauce on top of the fish, and add a third of the grated cheese.

Add 4 more lasagne sheets, then the remaining fish mixture. Top with another third of the sauce and a third of the cheese. Finally, add your last layer of lasagne sheets, the rest of the white sauce, and the remainder of the cheese. Pop into the oven and bake for 30–40 minutes.

SPECIAL BEEF CURRY
with Chapattis

I cook beef curries often, but there's one really special recipe that gets made just once a year, for a religious festival. When that time of year is approaching, I try to refrain from the everyday curries, so that the festival meal feels all the more special. Traditionally the pot boils away on the stove for hours. But I am so impatient that if I can make something I love in an eighth of the time, I will. So this is my simplified special beef curry, served with delicious fried chapattis.

SERVES 4, MAKES 12 CHAPPATTIS

PREP 40 MINS

COOK 1 HOUR

INGREDIENTS

For the beef curry
4 tbsp olive oil

3 cloves of garlic, peeled

30g fresh ginger, peeled and sliced

2 medium onions, finely chopped

1 tsp salt

½ tsp ground cinnamon

1 tsp chilli powder

2 tbsp garam masala

700g diced beef, ideally lean braising steak

500ml water

a large bunch of fresh chives, finely chopped

For the fried chapattis
500g plain flour, plus extra for dusting

½ tsp salt

2 tbsp olive oil

300ml warm water

vegetable oil, for frying

METHOD For the curry, put the oil, garlic, ginger, onions, salt, cinnamon, chilli powder and garam masala into a food processor and blitz to a smooth paste. Put a large non-stick saucepan on the hob on a high heat and add a glug of oil. When the oil is hot, add the paste and cook for 10 minutes, until the mixture begins to darken and thicken.

Now add the beef and mix it into the spices. Cook for 10 minutes, until the meat has browned on the outside. Stir in the water, then cover the pan and cook for 40 minutes on a low heat, until the meat is tender.

Meanwhile, make the chapatti dough. Put the flour in a bowl with the salt and oil. Add the water and bring together into a dough. Knead the dough in the bowl until it is smooth. It should feel stiff – this will help the chapattis to puff up in the oil.

Dust a work surface with flour. Take golf-ball sized pieces of dough and roll them out to thin rounds. Meanwhile, your oil can be heating up. Put a deep, wide-topped sauté pan on a medium heat and fill about one-third full with oil. The temperature of the oil should be about 180°C, if you are measuring exactly. Another way of testing is to drop a tiny pinch of spare dough into the oil and if it bubbles and rises to the surface the oil is ready.

Drop the dough rounds into the oil. You should be able to fry 2 at a time. They only need 3 minutes on each side. Using a slotted spoon, move each chapatti around gently, pressing the top lightly to get it to puff up.

Drain the chapattis upright in a colander, to allow any excess oil to drop out and steam to escape, which helps keep them crisp.

By now, the beef curry should be ready. Serve with chives sprinkled on top and the chapattis alongside

SERVES 4

PREP 15 MINS

COOK 30-40 MINS

I love standing by the stove and stirring while something cooks slowly and gently. Much like a classic rice risotto, this recipe takes time and attention. It cannot be rushed. Or can it? In this instance, yes, it can a bit, as bulgur wheat takes less time to cook than traditional risotto rice. Using bulgur also gives this risotto extra bite and nuttiness. Topped with crispy squid, and with garlic mayo stirred through, it's rich and a little bit special.

INGREDIENTS

For the bulgur wheat risotto

150ml vegetable oil

1 medium onion, finely diced

½ tsp salt

2 tsp cumin seeds

250g bulgur wheat

1.2 litres fish stock

4 tbsp full-fat mayonnaise

3 cloves of garlic, grated

For the crispy squid

4 tbsp vegetable oil

2 tbsp plain flour

a large pinch of salt

1 tbsp paprika

300g squid rings, uncooked

To serve

rocket leaves

juice of 1 lemon

olive oil

METHOD To make the risotto, put a large saucepan on the hob and turn the heat up to high. Pour the oil into the pan and when it's hot add the onion. Cook until crisp and very dark but not burned. You can encourage this by just letting the onion sit in the oil and not stirring too much. If it starts to darken around the edges, give it a stir and leave to brown. This should take at least 5 minutes.

As soon as the onion is very brown, add the salt and cumin seeds. Add the bulgur wheat and cook it for about 5 minutes in the mixture, stirring all the time. It will catch and feel dry at the bottom of the pan, but all this will add flavour.

Have the stock at the ready. Keeping the pan on a high heat, add a ladle of stock at a time. Once it has all been absorbed and has evaporated, add some more. Keep doing this until all the stock has been used up. This can take up to 10 or even 20 minutes of stirring, so persevere. I promise it will be worth it!

Once most of the stock has been absorbed, the little liquid that remains should be thick, not watery. Take off the heat.

Mix the mayonnaise with the garlic and stir it into the risotto – this will make it rich and creamy and give it a whopping garlic kick.

For the crispy squid, place a frying pan on a high heat and add the oil. Mix the flour with the salt and paprika. Toss the squid in the flour mixture until all the rings are coated. Fry them in the hot oil in batches, making sure not to overcrowd the pan, then drain on kitchen paper. They should only take a few minutes on each side.

Serve the risotto topped with rocket leaves, a squeeze of lemon, a drizzle of oil and with the crispy squid rings on top.

SQUID BULGUR RISOTTO
with Blackened Onions and Garlic Aïoli

Squid bulgur risotto

blackened onions, garlic aïoli,

crispy squid, squeeze of lemon,

rich and special,

whopping garlic kick

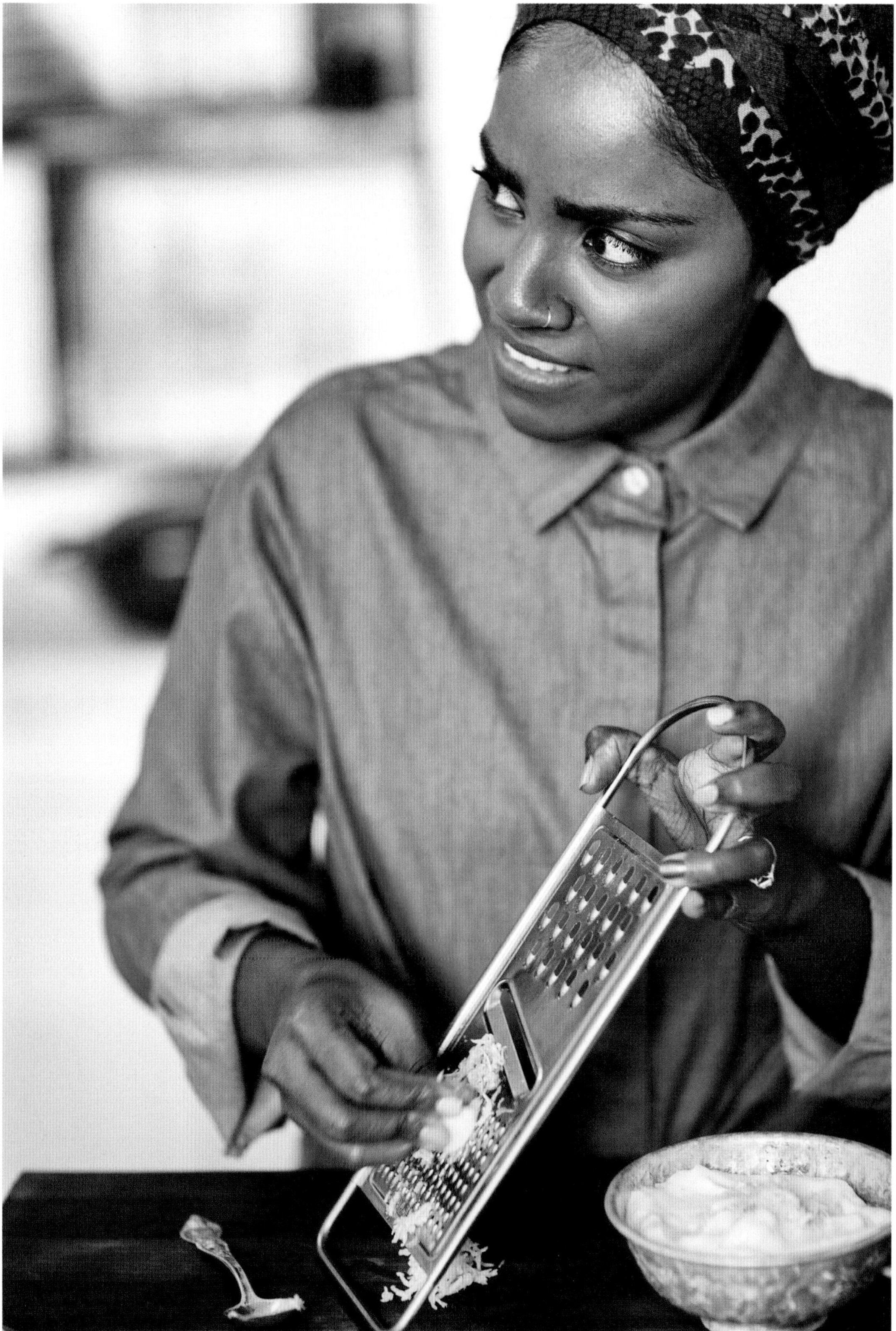

I love a bit of fusion cooking, and this is fusion at its best. I first ate this at my beautiful friend Ani's house, and it was so delicious I had to recreate it. A simple curry, minus traditional paneer – because I don't always have paneer in the fridge at home and many supermarkets only sell halloumi. (The need to improvise is how the best recipes are often created!). The bonus here is the spicy coconutty sambal, which gets sprinkled on top at the end. This one's for my girl Ani.

SERVES **4**

PREP **20 MINS**

COOK **35 MINS**

INGREDIENTS

For the curry

4 tbsp olive oil

2 x 250g blocks of halloumi cheese, cut into 1cm cubes

6 cloves of garlic, chopped

2 red onions, diced

2 red peppers, diced

½ tsp salt

½ tsp ground turmeric

1 tsp cumin seeds

1 lemon, zest and juice

300ml water

a large bunch of fresh coriander, chopped

cooked basmati rice, to serve

For the sambal

150g desiccated coconut

1 clove of garlic

1 lime, zest and juice

a large handful of fresh coriander

to serve

basmati rice

METHOD To make the curry, put a large non-stick saucepan on a high heat and add 2 tablespoons of oil. Add the cubes of cheese and fry them, making sure to toss them around so they get a good browning all over. You may need to do this in 2 batches.

Spoon out the cheese and set aside on a plate. Add another 2 tablespoons of oil to the pan, then add the garlic and let it brown for a few minutes.

Add the onions, red peppers and salt and cook until they are soft – this will take about 10 minutes. Add the turmeric, cumin seeds, lemon zest and juice. Stir and cook for a few minutes, then pour in the water and cook for 10 minutes.

Take off the heat and use a stick blender to purée the mixture to a smooth paste.

Put the pan back on the heat and add the fried halloumi. Heat the cheese through and add the chopped coriander.

To make the sambal, put the coconut, garlic, lime juice and zest and coriander into a food processor and blitz until the mixture is an even texture.

Serve the curry with hot basmati rice, and sprinkle generously with the coconut sambal.

HALLOUMI CURRY
with Coconut Sambal

SERVES 4

PREP 30 MINS,
PLUS RISING

COOK 15-20 MINS

INGREDIENTS

For the dough
650g strong bread flour,
plus extra for dusting

7g fast-action yeast

10g salt

25ml olive oil

375ml warm water

For the topping
500g passata

1 tsp dried oregano

a good pinch of salt

16 slices of pepperoni

150g mozzarella balls
(drained weight)

200g Cheddar cheese,
grated

50g garlic butter, melted

12 fresh basil leaves

I came across the craze for pizza pot pies while watching an American food show. I always think Amercian recipes shout, 'Go big or go home,' and this recipe does just that! It's about being the daddy of the deep pan. It is quite literally a pizza in an edible dough bowl. It can't get much bigger than that – or can it?

METHOD First make the dough. Put the flour into a bowl, with the yeast on one side and the salt on the other. (If the two touch, the salt will kill the yeast. They can mix later, but at that stage the flour will act as a barrier.)

Make a well in the centre and add the oil and water. If you are using a stand mixer, attach a dough hook, then mix and knead for 5 minutes on a high speed. If you are doing it by hand, bring the dough together and knead it on a work surface (dusting with a little flour) for 10 minutes. The dough is ready when it is smooth and elastic and shiny.

Pop the dough back into the bowl and cover. Leave in a warm place for 1 hour, or until it has doubled in size. Meanwhile make the filling.

Mix the passata with the oregano and salt and set aside.

Preheat the oven to 220°C/200°C fan/gas mark 7. You will need 4 19.5cm pie dishes or ovenproof dishes of similar size. In each dish place 4 pieces of pepperoni. Divide the mozzarella balls among the 4 dishes, about 4–5 balls per dish. Add equal amounts of the grated cheese, about 50g per dish, then spoon the passata on top.

Once the dough has doubled in size, knock it back and deflate it. Give it a quick knead and divide it into 4 equal amounts.

Roll out each piece of dough so it is large enough to cover the base and sides of the pie dish with plenty of overhang, then use the rolled-out pieces to line each dish. Pierce each dough bowl once with a sharp knife, to allow steam to escape. Brush all over with the melted garlic butter.

Place the dishes on 2 baking trays and bake for 15–20 minutes, until the dough is golden brown. Swap the position of the trays halfway through.

Once baked, brush with the garlic butter again. One at a time, put a plate on top of each pie. Hold tight and flip it over, then prise the dish off carefully. I would use oven gloves or a thick tea towel, as it will be very hot. What you should get is an avalanche of cheese and tomato. Tear up the basil and sprinkle on top.

As trends go, this is a new family favourite. Thank you, America!

SERVES 4-5

PREP 20 MINS

COOK 30 MINS

When I was younger, I had a brother and sister, Jak and Pink, who spent a lot of time in and out of hospital, so life was tailored around their hospital stays. The best times were when they came home after operations, when my parents would make them special food. Of course I was pleased to see my siblings home, but I also secretly loved that they never finished their meals, and I was always willing to help with that. My dad would make the creamiest instant mash and I used to wait with bated breath for my turn. Now, when my pups are poorly, that's what I make for them: the creamiest homemade mash with delicious tomato soup.

INGREDIENTS

*For the soup
(makes 800ml)*

10 tomatoes
(about 850g)

3 tbsp olive oil

2 cloves of garlic,
chopped

1 tsp sugar

1 tsp salt

1 tsp chilli flakes

1 tsp tomato purée

2 tbsp Worcestershire
sauce

1 slice of white bread,
torn into chunks

20ml double cream

2 tbsp chopped fresh
chives, to serve

For the mash

900g floury potatoes
such as Maris Pipers,
peeled and quartered

1 tsp salt

50g unsalted butter

100ml double cream

3 tbsp full-fat
mayonnaise

METHOD Pop the potatoes into a pan of cold water and boil them for about 15–20 minutes, or until tender.

For the soup, cut a slit in the skin of each tomato and put them into a heatproof bowl. Pour over boiling water, then cover the bowl with clingfilm and set aside for the skins to loosen. This should only take about 10 minutes. Drain the tomatoes, peel away the skins, and roughly chop.

Put a medium pan on a medium heat. Add the oil and when it's hot add the garlic. As the garlic gets brown, add the chopped tomatoes.

Add the sugar, salt, chilli flakes, tomato purée and Worcestershire sauce. Pop in the torn bread, then cook it all on a medium heat for 10 minutes.

Using a stick blender, blend the soup to a smooth paste. Stir in the cream, then keep the soup warm while you make the mash.

Drain the potatoes and mash with a ricer or a potato masher. Add the salt, butter, cream and mayonnaise and mix until smooth.

To serve, it's simple – a massive mound of mash and the soup poured all around, topped with a sprinkling of chives.

CREAMY MASH with Tomato Soup

This savoury traybake recipe gives me so much joy. All the magic happens in the oven, leaving no mess to clear up on the stove. Because the rice is cooked in the tray, you end up with lovely toasted bits as well as fluffy grains. And the chicken, rubbed with spices, is cooked right on top. All it needs is the family to eat it, and they are never too far away.

SERVES 4

PREP 15 MINS

COOK 55-60 MINS

INGREDIENTS

For the rice

oil, for greasing

1 large onion, finely diced

3 cloves of garlic, chopped

50g clarified butter, melted (or butter)

270g basmati rice

2 cardamom pods, seeds only

650ml hot chicken stock (or boiling water)

200g frozen peas

a large handful of fresh coriander, chopped

For the chicken

8 chicken drumsticks, with skin on

2 tbsp oil

1 tsp salt

1 tsp garlic powder

1 tsp onion powder

1 tsp cayenne pepper

METHOD Preheat the oven to 200°C/180°C fan/gas mark 6. Lightly grease a large roasting tray and put in the onion and garlic. Drizzle over the melted butter and give the onion a stir. Bake for 10–15 minutes, making sure it doesn't begin to burn. Keep an eye on it – if the edges are catching too quickly, take the tray out and give it all another stir before putting it back in.

While the onion is cooking, rub the drumsticks with the oil and mix the salt, garlic, onion and cayenne in a bowl. Cover the drumsticks all over with the spicy rub.

Take out the tray of onion and add the rice and cardamom seeds. Stir the rice into the onion mix and put the drumsticks on top. Pour in the stock. Cover with foil and bake for 30 minutes.

Take out of the oven, lift the chicken drumsticks on to a side plate, then add the peas to the rice and lightly stir them through. Replace the chicken pieces and bake without the foil for another 15 minutes.

Stir in the chopped coriander and serve.

CHICKEN AND RICE BAKE

SERVES 4

PREP 25 MINS

COOK 1 HOUR

Chicken breast is a staple in our house, especially for feeding the kids. It's quick and easy and, most importantly, versatile. I never seem to have breadcrumbs when I need them, but what I always have plenty of is wheat biscuit breakfast cereal, and that's how these escalopes were born. They're rather like big homemade chicken nuggets, served with hazelnut mashed potato and pink pickled red onions.

INGREDIENTS

For the hazelnut mash

1kg floury potatoes such as Maris Pipers, peeled and quartered

100g butter

1 tsp salt

3 tbsp full-fat mayonnaise

100g chopped roasted hazelnuts

For the quick pickled onions

300ml apple cider vinegar

2 red onions, sliced

For the escalopes

4 chicken breasts

2 tsp salt

2 tsp cayenne pepper

2 eggs, beaten

4 wheat cereal biscuits, crushed

5 tbsp olive oil

1 tbsp butter

METHOD Pop the prepared potatoes into a large saucepan of cold water, then place on a high heat and cook for 15–20 minutes, or until the potatoes are tender.

Get the pickle going by putting the vinegar into a pan with the onions. Place on a high heat and bring to the boil, then lower the heat and leave to simmer until the onions are soft. This can take about 30 minutes. Open a window, as the smell can get potent!

While the potatoes boil and the onions pickle, get started on the chicken breasts. Butterfly them by cutting across the breast horizontally, but not cutting all the way through, and opening the breast up. Use the back of your hand to flatten it as much as possible. Once you have done that to all 4 breasts, sprinkle them with the salt and cayenne pepper, making sure to pat it in everywhere.

Have 2 plates ready, one with the eggs and the other with the crushed wheat biscuits. Dip each breast first into the egg and then into the crushed wheat biscuits. Set aside on a plate.

By now the potatoes should be done. Drain them, then pop them back into the pan and mash them using a potato masher or a ricer. Add the butter, salt and mayonnaise and mix, then stir in the roasted hazelnuts.

Back to the chicken. Get a large non-stick frying pan and place it on a medium heat. If you have a pan large enough, you may be able to cook 2 at a time, which is how I do it, using my largest frying pan.

Add the oil and butter to the pan. When the butter has melted, add 2 of the escalopes and fry for 4–6 minutes on each side, until the chicken is cooked through. Remove from the pan, then fry the other 2 escalopes.

Drain off the vinegar from the onions and rinse them with warm water. Serve the hot chicken with the mash and the pickled red onions.

WHEAT ESCALOPES
with Hazelnut Mash and Pink Pickled Onions

My eldest son, Musa, was allergic to aubergines for a few years, so we had to stop using them. But when you know you can't eat something, of course you want it even more, and during that time I was always like a bandit on the lookout for aubergines, desperate to sneak a taste wherever I could. Then one day, we discovered he'd grown out of the allergy. I immediately went and bought aubergines and made a huge moussaka, crammed with even more aubergine than normal. Now it's one of his favourites!

SERVES **6**

PREP **25 MINS**

COOK **1 HOUR**

INGREDIENTS

5 tbsp olive oil

1 cinnamon stick

7 cloves of garlic, chopped

1 small red onion, finely chopped

2 tomatoes, chopped

1½ tsp salt

1 tbsp tomato purée

1 lemon, zest and juice

½ tsp chilli powder

1 tsp ground cumin

3 large aubergines, cubed

a small handful of fresh parsley, chopped

For the topping
500g ricotta

a pinch of salt

1 tsp freshly ground black pepper

170g Cheddar cheese, finely grated

1 egg yolk

To serve
green salad and garlic bread

METHOD Put a large saucepan on a high heat. Add the oil to the pan and when it is hot add the cinnamon and garlic. When the garlic is brown, add the onion, tomato, salt and tomato purée and cook for about 10 minutes, or until the onion is soft.

Add the lemon zest and juice, chilli powder and cumin and cook for a few minutes.

Add the diced aubergines. I like keeping the skin on – it means the aubergines don't turn to mush and they hold their shape better. Stir so that the aubergines are coated all over, then cover the pan and leave to cook on a medium to low heat. This should only take 10–15 minutes. Just be sure to stir them occasionally, to make sure nothing is sticking to the bottom of the pan. Then you will know whether to adjust the heat or not.

The base is ready when the aubergines are cooked. They should look waterlogged almost, like they have soaked up all the juices from everything around them. They should be brown rather than the stark white they were when they went in. Take off the heat and stir in the parsley, then put the aubergine mix into a 20 x 30cm casserole dish. Don't forget to fish out that cinnamon stick! It has done its job, and nobody needs to find a stick in their food, unless it's April Fool's.

Preheat the oven to 220°C/200°C fan/gas mark 7.

To make the topping, put the ricotta into a bowl with the salt, pepper, two-thirds of the cheese and the egg yolk. Mix well, then spread all over the top of the aubergines. Sprinkle over the rest of the cheese and bake for 30 minutes on the middle shelf of the oven.

We love to eat this with a really simple green salad and some garlic bread, the frozen baguette variety!

Something sweet

There is one member of my family who doesn't have a sweet tooth. Even after a meal. Who is she and how are we related? The rest of us will stampede over each other to find something sweet. We search cupboards, jars, even raid the kids' stashes. We just need something sweet! I have tried my best to resist those sugary urges, but I've never been grown-up enough to survive without. Even when I'm out, I always carry an emergency supply of midget gems to tide me over until I can go home and properly satisfy my craving. It doesn't have to be much, perhaps a small chunk of Apple Rocky Road, or a Carrot Cake Pakora from the night before. A scoop of Cookie Dough Ice Cream or a bite-size Syrup Sponge on my way out of the kitchen. Just something for a little sweet satisfaction! Here are the recipes that keep us sane. All except one of us, who can happily go without.

MAKES 18 BARS

PREP 20 MINS,
PLUS CHILLING

COOK 5 MINS

Rocky road, minus the marshmallows, was one of the first things I ever made with my children. Twelve years ago, finding halal or even vegetarian marshmallows was tricky, so even simple recipes like this felt like quite a challenge. But now alternative ingredients are much more widely available, and I can even get halal and veggie marshmallows in most big-brand supermarkets. This apple rocky road has all the loveliness of a rocky road, but with a difference: squidgy marshmallow, sweet white chocolate, tart dried apples and fruity sultanas. A little bit goes a long way. But a little bit is better than none at all!

INGREDIENTS

200g white chocolate
(or chocolate chips)

2 tbsp golden syrup

130g unsalted butter,
plus extra for greasing

a pinch of salt

½ tsp ground cinnamon

200g cinnamon biscuits
(or digestives)

100g white mini
marshmallows (if you
can only find big
marshmallows, use
scissors to chop them
into small pieces)

100g dried apples,
chopped into small pieces

50g raisins

1 tbsp icing sugar, for
dusting

METHOD Lightly grease the inside of a 23cm square baking tin, then line the base and sides of the tin with baking paper.

Put about 2.5cm of water into a medium saucepan. Find a heatproof bowl that will fit into the top of the pan snugly. Make sure the base of the bowl doesn't touch the water, because this can scald the chocolate.

Put the pan on the stove and turn it up to a high heat. As soon as the water is boiling, turn it down low.

Chop the chocolate, or alternatively use chocolate chips. Put the chocolate into the bowl with the golden syrup and butter. Stir occasionally, making sure to agitate the chocolate, as this will encourage the mixture to melt and come together.

As soon as the mixture is smooth, liquid and runny, take off the heat and allow to cool for about 10 minutes. If it's too hot when the marshmallows are added, there will be a sticky mess.

Add the salt and cinnamon and mix through.

Crush the biscuits very roughly, by putting them into a freezer bag and crushing them here and there with a rolling pin. Empty the contents of the bag into the chocolate mix. Give it a stir.

Now add the marshmallows, apples and raisins and stir, making sure everything is well coated.

Pour the mixture into the prepared tin, then, using the back of a spoon, really go to work to flatten it and press it into the corners. Put the tin into the fridge for at least 1 hour, or until it has set.

Take out of the tin and unwrap. Dust with the icing sugar and slice into 18 bars, or choose your own size according to your sweet tooth.

APPLE ROCKY ROAD

CARROT CAKE PAKORAS
with Cream Cheese Dip

This is one those crazy ideas I get in the middle of the night. One of those ideas I'm so impatient to try that it draws me out of the comfort of my warm bed and down to the kitchen to start testing it right away, no matter what time it is! Imagine a carrot cake, with carrots, spices, nuts and raisins, but deep-fried, hot and dusted with icing sugar. All served with a cool sweet cream cheese dip. Now tell me that isn't worth the lack of sleep!

MAKES **20** PAKORAS

PREP **20 MINS**

COOK **15 MINS**

INGREDIENTS

For the dip

100g full-fat cream cheese

100g unsalted butter, room temperature

4 tbsp icing sugar

2 tbsp maple syrup, plus extra for drizzling

a pinch of salt

a pinch of mixed spice

METHOD These pakoras are best eaten fresh and warm, so I like to make the dip first so that it's ready and waiting. Mix the cream cheese and butter until smooth and fully combined, with no lumps.

Mix in the icing sugar, maple syrup and salt, then transfer into a serving bowl. Drizzle over a squirt of maple syrup and sprinkle with a pinch of mixed spice. Cover the bowl and pop into the fridge.

Put a medium pan (one that has a lid, in case you need to put the lid on in an emergency) on a high heat and add about 1.5 litres of oil, depending on the size of the pan – the oil needs to be halfway up.

Have a baking tray ready, lined with kitchen paper to soak up excess oil.

To start the pakoras, put the carrots, walnuts and raisins into a mixing bowl. Mix well.

Add the flour, baking powder, sugar, mixed spice and salt, and stir into the carrot mixture so everything is coated. Add the beaten eggs and keep mixing until you have a thick batter.

For the pakoras

1.5–2 litres vegetable oil

300g carrots
(3–4 medium ones),
peeled and grated

50g walnuts,
roughly chopped

50g raisins

120g self-raising flour

½ tsp baking powder

20g caster sugar

1 tsp mixed spice

½ tsp salt

2 medium eggs,
lightly beaten

up to 1 tbsp icing sugar,
for dusting

Test that the oil is hot enough by adding a tiny drop of the batter to the oil. If it sizzles and rises to the top, the oil is ready for frying. (If you're one of the few people who owns a cooking thermometer, this would be 170°C.) Turn the heat down to medium.

Using 2 teaspoons, one to pick up and the other to push out, gently drop teaspoons of the mixture into the oil. Work in batches, making sure not to overcrowd the pan.

Fry for about 4–5 minutes, moving them around and turning them occasionally so they are an even colour. They should be golden brown on the outside.

Remove the pakoras from the oil with a slotted spoon and drain on the paper-covered tray.

Fry more batches until all the batter is used up. Dust with icing sugar and serve with the dip. Hot fried cake, cool dip, and none of the waiting. Pakoras have taken on a whole new meaning.

I like my crumble with more fruit and less crumble, but I am outnumbered in my house where this is concerned, as they all like it the other way round. So these are just for me: individual pears poached, then baked with a sweet marzipan centre and a crumbly, crunchy top. You would have thought this would be enough to put the others off, but it turns out my lot will eat anything, regardless of fruit-to-crumble ratio!

SERVES 6

PREP 15 MINS

COOK 50 MINS

INGREDIENTS

For the pears

3 large pears, peeled and halved

500ml apple juice

1 vanilla pod, split

150g demerara sugar

75g golden marzipan

For the crumble

50g plain flour

25g unsalted butter

25g demerara sugar

100g granola

To serve

ice cream

METHOD Put the pears into a medium saucepan with the apple juice and vanilla pod, making sure to scrape out the vanilla seeds into the apple juice. Boil the pears in the juice for 20–30 minutes, until they are tender.

Preheat the oven to 200°C/180°C fan/gas mark 6 and have a roasting dish or baking tray at the ready, large enough to fit all 6 pear halves.

Once the pears are poached, take them out of the pan, leaving the poaching liquid behind, and drain them on kitchen paper. Remove the vanilla pod from the poaching liquid and add the demerara sugar, then bring to the boil on a high heat and reduce the juice till it is thick and syrupy.

To make the crumble, put the flour and butter into a bowl. Rub in the butter with the tips of your fingers until the mixture looks like breadcrumbs. Mix in the sugar and granola.

Once the pears have cooled, use a teaspoon to take out the core from each one. Place the pear halves in the roasting dish and fill the cavities with chunks of marzipan.

Pat the crumble on top of each pear half and bake in the oven for 20 minutes.

As soon as the pears are ready, take them out and serve hot. The juice should have reduced by now, so drizzle it all over the pears and serve with a massive dollop of ice cream.

HALF-A-PEAR CRUMBLE

MAKES **APPROX. 35**

PREP **35 MINS**

COOK **20 MINS**

INGREDIENTS

For the filling
60g desiccated coconut

20g pistachios, crushed

5 tbsp clarified butter

20g brown sugar

1 tsp whole fennel seeds,
lightly crushed

For the pastry
300g plain flour, plus
extra for dusting

200ml cold water

1.5 litres vegetable oil

salt, for sprinkling

For the cocktail dip
1 x 415g tin of fruit
cocktail in juice, drained

1 tbsp icing sugar

1 lime, zest and juice

1 lemon, zest and juice

These are my favourite celebration treats. My nan always made them for pregnant women in the family as a gift in their final weeks of pregnancy, a tradition special to our family even today. All I'm saying is that you don't have to be with child to enjoy these, with their crisp pastry and sweet coconut filling. I like to serve them with a zesty, fruity cocktail dip. Any leftovers are great frozen and later reheated in the oven.

METHOD Start by making the filling, so it has time to cool before being used. Put the coconut, pistachios, butter, sugar and fennel seeds into a small non-stick pan. On a medium heat, warm the mixture until the butter has melted, then cook for another 5 minutes, until the coconut has plumped up and the mixture is really dry. Take off the heat and transfer to a bowl to cool.

For the pastry, put the flour into a bowl and make a well in the centre. Add the water, and mix in using a dinner knife. Then get your hands in and bring the dough together in the bowl, making sure to grab any dry bits of flour. Cover with clingfilm and set aside for a few minutes.

Meanwhile, make the dip. Drain the fruit cocktail through a sieve, removing as much liquid as possible. Put the fruit in a small food processor or into a jug if you are using a hand-held blender. Add the icing sugar and the juice and zest of the lime and lemon and blend the mixture to a smooth paste. Pass it through the sieve again to make sure it's really smooth, then cover with clingfilm and set aside. If you are making the dip in advance, put it into the fridge (bring back to room temperature before serving).

Have a large baking tray ready, dusted with a little flour. Sprinkle flour on your worktop and roll out the pastry to about 3mm thick. Using a 6.5cm cutter, cut out as many circles as you can, then gather up any spare pastry and roll it out again. Keep cutting out circles until you have no pastry left.

Place a teaspoon of filling on to each circle, positioning it on one side. Use up all the filling. Fold the other half of each circle over the filling and crimp the edges, using the tip of a fork to press and seal. As each samosa is ready, place it on the prepared tray. Line another tray with kitchen paper.

Put the oil into a large pan on a high heat. (If you use a thermometer, the oil should be at 180°C, or test it by dropping a tiny bit of pastry into the pan – if it rises to the surface, the oil is ready.) Lower the heat to medium and fry the samosas in batches for 4–5 minutes, moving them all the time, until golden brown. Drain on the paper and sprinkle each batch with salt.

Serve the samosas while still hot, with the cocktail dip.

COCONUT FENNEL SAMOSAS

Coconut fennel samosas

sweet filling, *crisp pastry, celebration*

treats, pistachios, *zesty*, fruity dip

COOKIE DOUGH ICE CREAM

To me, ice cream has always been something you eat alongside something else. Cake with ice cream. Crumble with ice cream. Ice cream sundae. Ice cream in milkshake. Ice cream floats. But my kids just eat ice cream neat, in a bowl, with nothing else. So this is a recipe for a dessert that sits in the freezer, for whenever they want to eat JUST ice cream. I still look for things to put on it, under it or with it, though, so this simple vanilla ice cream has chunks of chocolate-chip cookie dough mixed through, making it perfect for them and for me.

SERVES 5

PREP 25 MINS,
PLUS FREEZING

NO COOK

INGREDIENTS

For the cookie dough
100g unsalted butter,
room temperature

175g soft brown sugar

1 tsp vanilla bean paste

2 tbsp whole milk

100g plain flour

40g cocoa powder

a large pinch of salt

100g dark chocolate
chips

For the ice cream
600ml double cream

6 tbsp golden syrup

1 tbsp vanilla bean paste

3 tbsp icing sugar

1 tbsp cocoa

METHOD Start by making the cookie dough. This is a no-cook dough. Cream the butter and sugar in a bowl, using a hand-held mixer, until the mixture is light and fluffy. Mix in the vanilla paste and milk.

Add the flour, cocoa and salt and beat until your dough begins to come together into a ball. Then add the chocolate chips and use a spatula to mix them in so they are well dispersed.

Place the dough between two sheets of baking paper and roll it out to about 1cm thick. Place on a tray and put into the freezer while you make the ice cream.

Before starting the ice cream, have a 1 litre airtight freezer-safe container ready. You will also need a zip-lock freezer bag that is big enough to house the container.

Put the cream and golden syrup into a mixing bowl and whisk until the cream forms stiff peaks. This should take a few minutes. Then add the vanilla, icing sugar and cocoa and whisk again until you reach stiff peaks.

Take the cookie dough out of the freezer. Remove the top layer of baking paper and cut the dough into 1cm cubes.

Take two-thirds of the cookie dough cubes and fold them into the cream. Pour the mixture into the ice cream tub, level off the surface, then add the rest of the cookie dough on top.

Pop the lid on and put the tub into the zip-lock bag. Seal the bag and freeze for a minimum of 4 hours.

This is enough for my family of 5 to polish off in one sitting. I'm just saying . . . it might not make it back to the freezer.

CRANBERRY BREAD PUDDING

I always have more bread in the house than I need. Shop-bought, homemade, reduced-aisle yellow-sticker loaves, always far too much. Even after giving some to my mum I usually still have too much, and there's only so much enthusiasm the neighbours can show for sliced bread. So this is a recipe I created as a way of using it up and giving it away in a different form. The stale white bread is dotted with delicious red cranberries, and makes a fresher alternative to an old classic.

SERVES 12

PREP 40 MINS,
PLUS SOAKING

COOK 1 HOUR
45 MINS

INGREDIENTS

500g white bread
(stale bread works best)

110g dried cranberries,
finely chopped

1 satsuma, peel only,
pith removed, very
thinly sliced

600ml whole milk

2 large eggs

140g caster sugar

1 tsp vanilla bean paste

100g butter, melted,
plus extra for greasing

2 tbsp demerara sugar

½–1 tbsp icing sugar

METHOD Lightly grease and line a 23cm round cake tin, ideally not one with a loose bottom.

Break the bread into a food processor and whiz till you have fine bread-crumbs. Put the breadcrumbs into a large bowl with the dried cranberries and satsuma peel.

Pour the milk into a saucepan and bring to the boil, then turn off the heat.

Put the eggs, sugar and vanilla bean paste into a smaller bowl and whisk until the mixture is light and fluffy. Slowly add the warm milk in a steady stream, making sure to whisk all the time. Keep adding the milk until it is all used up.

Pour the milk mixture into the bowl of breadcrumbs. Stir, then leave aside for 30 minutes for the crumbs to soak up the mixture.

After 30 minutes, pour the melted butter into the bread mixture. Stir, then spoon the mixture into the prepared tin.

Sprinkle with the demerara sugar and bake in the preheated oven for 1 hour 30 minutes to 1 hour 45 minutes. If you find it is browning too much, cover with foil halfway through baking.

When you take it out of the oven, leave it to cool completely in the tin.

Once cool, remove from the tin and dust with icing sugar, then cut. I like to go completely unconventional and cut it into squares. I know because it is made in a round tin this means there is inequality in the size of the slices, but first come, first served, I say.

MAKES **APPROX.**
64 PIECES

PREP **15 MINS,**
PLUS CHILLING

COOK **10 MINS**

There are two ways of making fudge – the harder way and the easier way. I love making it the lengthier way, boiling sugar and cream. But the easy way is quicker and more reliable. This is my easy recipe, made with almond butter, which creates fudge that is crunchy, sweet and salty in one bite. Perfect kept in a jar in the kitchen for every time you need a sweet hit.

INGREDIENTS

125g unsalted butter, plus extra for greasing

500g soft dark brown sugar

120ml whole milk

250g crunchy almond butter

1 vanilla pod, seeds scraped out

½ tsp rock salt, plus extra for sprinkling

300g icing sugar, sifted

50g flaked almonds

METHOD Lightly grease a 23 cm square cake tin and line with baking paper.

Melt the butter in a medium saucepan on a medium heat. Add the sugar and milk and bring to the boil, then give it a stir to combine and cook for about 3 minutes. If you are using a sugar thermometer it should read 115°C. While it's boiling, make sure not to stir, just swirl the pan occasionally to make sure nothing is sticking to the base.

Take the pan off the heat and add the almond butter, vanilla seeds and rock salt, then mix till everything is combined well.

Put the icing sugar into a bowl. Pour in the hot mixture and stir until the fudge is a smooth even paste.

Pour into the prepared tin and level off the surface, using the back of a spoon.

Crush the flaked almonds in the palms of your hands and put the pieces into a small non-stick frying pan on a high heat, making sure to stir occasionally. What you want is for the smaller pieces to begin to burn and the bigger bits to toast really well.

Scatter the almonds over the fudge and sprinkle on some rock salt.

Put into the fridge till set, then take out of the tin and cut into tiny squares.

BURNT ALMOND BUTTER FUDGE

SERVES 6

PREP 15 MINS,
PLUS SOAKING

COOK 45 MINS

Whoever came up with the name 'yum yums' was not wrong! They are twisted bits of pastry that are first fried, then doused in a sugary water icing. And in this pudding I've taken something that is already delicious to another realm of yumminess, covering the yum yums with a creamy custard and adding the tang of dried apricots. Yum yums just got a tiny bit yummier.

INGREDIENTS

25g unsalted butter, melted, plus extra for greasing

8 yum yums, each sliced into 4 pieces

100g dried apricots, chopped

1 lemon, zest only

350ml whole milk

50ml double cream

2 large eggs

20g granulated sugar, plus extra for sprinkling

1 tbsp icing sugar, for dusting

pouring cream, to serve

METHOD Grease a medium casserole dish.

Put the yum yums into a large bowl and pour over the melted butter. Toss them around until the butter has coated them all.

Spread half the yum yums over the base of the casserole dish. Add the chopped apricots and sprinkle over the lemon zest. Put the rest of the yum yums on top.

Heat the milk and cream in a pan, taking it off the heat just before it starts to boil.

Put the eggs and sugar into a bowl and whisk until they are well combined. Slowly pour in the hot milk, making sure to whisk all the time.

Pour the warm custard into the casserole dish, on top of the yum yum/ apricot mix. Leave to sit for 30 minutes, so that all the custard can soak in.

Preheat the oven to 180°C/160°C fan /gas mark 4. Sprinkle over a little extra sugar and bake for 30–40 minutes, until the top is crisp and the custard has set.

I like to leave it in the dish for 10 minutes, then dust it with a little icing sugar and serve with pouring cream. Yum yum!

One of the big supermarkets used to sell these, in chocolate and strawberry varieties. At the time I had no clue what they were, so I bought some to find out. Thank goodness I had no expectations, as they didn't taste good. But that bad first impression made me determined to create a much better homemade version. And here it is: a chocolate and peanut pie filled with jam and marshmallow, like a cakey sandwich biscuit. The ultimate portable sweet treat!

MAKES 18 PIES

PREP 25 MINS

COOK 15 MINS

INGREDIENTS

For the pie

125g unsalted butter, softened

150g dark chocolate, chopped (or chocolate chips)

225g caster sugar

3 medium eggs

1 tsp vanilla extract

250g plain flour

30g cocoa powder

½ tsp baking powder

150g salted peanuts, roughly chopped

For the filling

18 medium white marshmallows

125g seedless raspberry jam

METHOD Preheat the oven to 200°C/180°C fan/gas mark 6. Line 2 baking trays with baking paper.

Put the butter and chocolate into a small bowl and melt in the microwave in 30-second bursts until the mixture is liquid. Set aside to cool.

Put the sugar, eggs and vanilla into the bowl of a stand mixer and whisk until the mixture is light, fluffy and doubled in volume. Add the cooled chocolate mixture and whisk quickly until combined.

Sift in the flour, cocoa and baking powder. Combine the mixture using the beaters until you have a smooth cake dough.

Take heaped tablespoons and create 36 mounds. Space them about 2.5cm apart and wet your fingers to pat each mound into a round shape. Sprinkle them with the chopped peanuts and bake for 8–10 minutes.

Take out of the oven and leave the oven on. Leave the pies to cool on the tray for about 10 minutes, giving them enough time to hold their shape a little.

Put 18 pies on to a cooling rack and leave the other 18 on the tray. Turn the ones on the tray over so the flat side is facing up.

Put a marshmallow on top of each one and put back into the oven until the marshmallows have softened – about 1–2 minutes. If the marshmallows are very soft, leave them to firm a little before sandwiching, otherwise the top and bottom will slide apart.

Spread a teaspoon of jam on the other 18 pie halves and sandwich them with the marshmallow halves.

I like to give the marshmallow a few minutes to set before eating, else it oozes out the sides. But if you like the ooze, eat them fast.

CHOCOLATE, JAM AND
PEANUT WHOOPIE PIES

MAKES APPROX.
16 BAKES

PREP 30 MINS,
PLUS COOLING

COOK 1 HOUR
25 MINS

There is a traditional biscuit that all my uncles in Bangladesh eat for breakfast, and the same thing has made it overseas to us here in the UK, a hybrid biscuit-cake thing that you can buy in specialist grocers. I never understood the appeal, as to me they don't taste of anything, and some are so crunchy you fear losing your teeth and your hearing. So I decided to make a much nicer version, with less of the crunch and a lot more sweetness. This cake-crossed-with-biscuit is crisp, lemony and perfectly dunkable. I will make and transport these back to Bangladesh for my uncle's breakfast one day.

INGREDIENTS

For the cake
200g unsalted
butter, softened

200g caster sugar

4 medium eggs,
lightly beaten

1 lemon, zest only

200g self-raising
flour, sifted

1 tsp baking powder

For the syrup
200g caster sugar

40ml water

METHOD Preheat the oven to 180°C/160°C fan/gas mark 4. Grease the base of a 900g loaf tin and line it with baking paper.

Put all the cake ingredients into a mixing bowl. This is the all-in-one method, which can be a great time-saver. Mix for about 3 minutes, until the cake batter is smooth and shiny and well combined.

Spoon the batter into the prepared tin and level off the surface. Bake in the oven on the middle shelf for 40–45 minutes, until a skewer inserted comes out clean and the edges of the cake have come away from the sides of the tin.

Once baked, take it out of the oven but leave the oven turned on. Let the cake cool in the tin for 10 minutes, then remove it from the tin, take off the paper and leave to cool for another 10 minutes. The cooler the cake, the cleaner the cuts will be.

Have 2 baking trays ready. Slice the cake into 1cm thick slices. Lay the slices on their side on the baking trays and put them into the oven for another 20 minutes.

Take the trays out of the oven and turn the slices over. Pop them back into the oven for another 20 minutes.

Meanwhile make the syrup by combining the sugar and water.

Turn the oven off and take the trays out, then immediately cover one side of the crunchy cake biscuit things with the sugary syrup. Make sure to spread it all over. The fizzing, bubbling sound as the sugar hits the hot crisp bake is so much fun.

Leave for about 10 minutes before eating, as they will be very hot.

These keep in an airtight container for up to a month.

Bake
(biscuit-meets-cake)

crisp, *sweet*, lemony,

perfectly dunkable

SERVES 4-6

PREP 30 MINS

COOK 40 MINS

This recipe is for anyone who loves éclairs, but wishes they took less time to make. Of course, you could simply buy one from the shop and, believe me, when I need my fix I often do, and gobble it up before the kids can lay eyes on it. But for those who prefer their treats homemade, this is a safe place in between, offering all the great elements of an éclair – pastry, cream and chocolate – but with a little less work and time involved.

INGREDIENTS

For the choux pastry
200ml water

85g unsalted butter, plus extra for greasing

1 tbsp caster sugar

a pinch of salt

115g plain flour, sifted

3 medium eggs, beaten

For the filling
300ml whipping cream

2 tbsp icing sugar

1 tsp vanilla bean paste

4 tbsp salted caramel

For the ganache
200g dark chocolate

100ml double cream

100g milk chocolate, shaved

METHOD Preheat the oven to 200°C/180°C fan/gas mark 6. Lightly grease a baking tray and line it with baking paper.

Put the water, butter, sugar and salt into a pan on a medium to high heat. Just barely bring to the boil, so the sugar and butter dissolve. Once they have dissolved, turn the heat down and drop the flour in quickly in one go. Stir straight away and keep going, to avoid any lumps. The mixture should look smooth and be coming away from the sides of the pan as you mix it.

Take off the heat. Add the eggs a little at a time, mixing after each addition. The mixture will look like it is separating, but keep mixing and it will come together. Keep going until all the eggs are used and the dough is smooth.

Pour the mixture into the centre of the prepared tray. Using an offset spatula or the back of a spoon, spread the mixture to a rectangle shape, roughly 20 x 30cm. Wet your fingers and pat down any peaks that may have formed, then pop it into the oven for 30 minutes.

Have a clean tea towel ready for when you take out the pastry. Take the roll out of the oven and turn it out on to the tea towel. Roll up the pastry from the shorter end, using the tea towel to help – being sure to roll up the tea towel inside the pastry too. Leave for 20 minutes to cool.

To make the filling, whip the cream to soft peaks with the icing sugar and vanilla bean paste. For the ganache, chop the dark chocolate and put it into a bowl. Warm the cream in a small pan, being careful not to let it boil. As soon as it just begins to come up to the boil, take it off the heat and pour it on to the chocolate. Mix until the chocolate has melted completely.

Unroll the pastry and spread the cream all over. Drizzle over the salted caramel. Re-roll the pastry, starting from the shorter end as before (this time don't wrap up the tea towel – tea towels are not tasty).

Put the roll on a serving plate and spread the ganache on top. Sprinkle over the shavings of milk chocolate and leave in the fridge when you are not eating it. If it makes it to the fridge at all, that is!

ÉCLAIR ROLL

MAKES 54
SQUARES

PREP 15 MINS,
PLUS SETTING

NO COOK

I used to categorically loathe these as a child. I hated the flavour of the coconut. These days I will inhale anything edible that is out in front of me. As an adult I love coconut, and you really have to love coconut to love these . . . seeing as their main ingredient is coconut. I used to eat the pink layer hoping for a different flavour and it was all just the same. So I have given my pink layer a tiny twist by adding dehydrated strawberries. Now the pink actually tastes of something.

INGREDIENTS

14g freeze-dried strawberries

200g desiccated coconut

250g icing sugar, sifted

250g sweetened condensed milk

1 tbsp vanilla bean paste

METHOD Very lightly grease a 23cm square cake tin and line it with baking paper. Set aside.

In a mini food processor, blend the freeze-dried strawberries to a fine powder and put to one side for later.

Put the coconut and icing sugar into a large bowl and mix well. Add the condensed milk and mix by hand (I like to wear gloves) until the mixture is stiff and well combined.

Remove half the mixture to a separate bowl and add the vanilla bean paste to it. Get your hands in and mix it well. Pour or spoon into the prepared tin and use your hands or the back of a spoon to really compress the mixture.

To the remaining half of the mix, add the strawberry powder, and again mix really well until the mixture is pink. Pour or spoon into the tin on top of the white layer and pat down until it is compact.

Leave the mixture in the tin for a couple of hours, until no longer sticky, then take out and peel off the paper. Leave to dry further overnight, to get the cleanest cut, or just cut into small squares. These are great as gifts but they keep really well in an airtight jar for a month too.

STRAWBERRY COCONUT ICE

MAKES 20-22

PREP 30 MINS,
PLUS RESTING
AND CHILLING

COOK 25 MINS

INGREDIENTS

For the dough

225g milk powder

110g plain flour, plus
extra for dusting

½ tsp baking powder

½ tsp bicarbonate
of soda

4 cardamom pods, seeds
only, crushed

250ml whole milk, room
temperature

25g unsalted butter,
melted

1 medium egg yolk

200ml oil

15g pistachios,
roughly chopped

1 small orange, zest only

For the syrup

400g caster sugar

400ml water

a pinch of saffron

If you've ever tried Indian sweets, you will know they are eye-wateringly sweet, even for those with a very sweet tooth, like me. One of my favourites is a sticky delight called gulab jamun, little syrup sponge balls that typically come with far more syrup than cake. I've never understood who needs all that syrup, as it usually gets left behind, so I have created my own version, which involves less syrup, and therefore less waste. Mine aren't as sweet as the traditional ones, but they're still sticky, spongy and very yummy.

METHOD Start by making the dough. Mix together the milk powder, plain flour, baking powder, bicarb and crushed cardamom seeds in a bowl. Mix together the milk, butter and egg yolk in another bowl.

Make a well in the centre of the flour mixture and add the wet mixture. Using a palette knife, bring it all together. The dough will be very wet. Cover and leave to one side for 30–40 minutes, so the milk powder can absorb some of the liquid.

Have a baking tray ready to put your prepared dough on. Lightly oil your hands to help prevent sticking. Take a piece of dough about the size of a walnut (in its shell), about 25g, and pack it into a tight ball. Repeat with the rest of the dough, placing the balls on the baking tray as you go. If the dough is sticking to your hands, wash them and rub them with a little more oil. Once the balls are on the tray, squash them a little to flatten them.

Now make the syrup. Put the sugar, water and saffron in a small pan on a high heat. Once it has boiled and the sugar has dissolved, take off the heat.

Put a large non-stick frying pan on a high heat and pour in the oil. Once it's hot, turn the heat down to medium.

Have a tray ready with kitchen paper, to mop up any extra oil. Gently drop the balls of dough into the oil. Fry for 2–3 minutes on one side, then turn them over and fry on the other side for another 2–3 minutes. They should be a lovely golden colour. Once fried, pop them on to the kitchen paper to drain.

Lay the balls out on a serving dish big enough that they can all be in a single layer. Spoon some of the reduced syrup on top of each ball of dough, then pour the rest of the syrup into the dish. Pop the dish into the fridge for 2 hours, for the syrup to soak in.

Before serving, sprinkle a little chopped pistachio and orange zest over each one. I like to eat these warmed in the microwave with a dollop of ice cream sometimes, but they are just as good served as they are.

SYRUP SPONGE BALLS

Soda bread is my go-to on a weekend. It's the fastest type of bread to make and eat. There is no kneading and no proving. Just mix, bake, sit back and wait long enough for it not to scald your mouth, then eat! Traditionally it's made in large loaves, but I'm treating this slightly differently and cooking it in a slab, with oozy caramel in the centre and lots of chocolate inside and on top.

MAKES **12 SQUARES**

PREP **20 MINS**

COOK **30 MINS**

INGREDIENTS

340g plain flour, plus extra for dusting

½ tsp bicarbonate of soda

25g caster sugar

½ tsp salt

100g dark chocolate, chopped (or chocolate chips)

290ml buttermilk (or 290ml whole milk, with 3 tbsp lemon juice mixed in)

1 tbsp vanilla bean paste

12 chocolate-covered caramels

1 tsp cocoa, for dusting

75g dark chocolate, melted

METHOD Preheat the oven to 200°C/180°C fan/gas mark 6. Have a baking tray ready and dusted with a little flour.

Put the flour, bicarb, sugar, salt and chocolate into a large bowl and mix together.

If you have buttermilk that's great, but if not you can make it using milk and lemon juice. If you leave the mixture for 5 minutes, it should thicken. Mix the vanilla paste into the buttermilk.

Make a well in the centre of the dry ingredients and add the wet ingredients, then use a palette knife to bring the dough together.

Drop the dough into the centre of the prepared baking tray. Using floured hands, flatten it to a square roughly 25 x 25cm.

Using a sharp knife, portion into 12 squares, making sure to cut all the way down. In the centre of each square add a soft caramel and push down gently into the centre.

Put the tray into the oven for 30 minutes.

Once the bread is baked, leave it on the tray for 10 minutes. Dust with cocoa and drizzle with the melted chocolate.

CARAMEL SODA BREAD TEAR AND SHARE

Cake

Everything in my life has a place. Shoes have their designated spot in the cloakroom. The vacuum cleaner has its place under the stairs. We even have set mealtimes for breakfast, lunch and dinner. And with that come rules. Cup of tea before breakfast. Savoury before sweet. Pasta sauce always mixed in, never on top. Rules, rules, rules! My kids will roll their eyes: they know I have a list of rules as long as my shopping receipts. I love rules. So what I'm about to say will surprise them. Cake, for me, should not have rules. It's important enough to be above all rules. Cake is a celebration, be it of birth, a new home or just because. Cake is a thank you covered in buttercream. Cake is what makes boring meetings bearable. Cake doesn't have to be for afters – if you want it first, have it first! Before dinner. Early in the morning. In the bath. Cake is in a league of its own. It's time to break the rules!

SERVES 8-10

PREP 25 MINS

COOK 1 HOUR
10 MINS

Streusel is the crunchy, crumbly bit on the top of this cake. That's my favourite part, although everything else below this delicious layer also makes it a really special treat, including the tart layer of soft apple with a hint of tarragon, and the layer of buttery sponge. Just like a surprise day off work, or finding £10 left in your raincoat pocket from last autumn, this is a *good day* kind of cake.

INGREDIENTS

For the streusel top
25g porridge oats
85g demerara sugar
50g unsalted butter
50g roasted hazelnuts

For the tarragon apple
2 tbsp unsalted butter
2 tbsp demerara sugar
4 green apples (about 640g), peeled, cored and chopped into chunks
a small handful of fresh tarragon, chopped (approx. 2 tbsp)

For the cake
100g unsalted butter, softened, plus extra for greasing
175g demerara sugar
2 medium eggs, lightly beaten
1 tsp vanilla extract
200g plain flour, sifted
2 tsp baking powder
100ml whole milk
1 tsp icing sugar, for dusting

METHOD Make the streusel top first by putting the oats, sugar, butter and hazelnuts into a small food processor and blitzing until well combined. Set aside for later.

Now make the apple mixture. Put the butter, sugar and prepared apples into a medium saucepan and cook for 8–10 minutes on a medium heat until the apples have softened. If you find they are getting mushy, take them off the heat sooner. They should be soft but still with some bite.

Once the apple pan is off the heat, add the tarragon and mix through. Transfer the apple mixture to a bowl so it can cool down before you add it to the cake.

Preheat the oven to 180°C/160°C fan/gas mark 4. Grease the base and sides of a 20cm round loose-bottomed cake tin and line with baking paper.

To make the cake, put the butter, sugar, eggs, vanilla, flour, baking powder and milk into a large mixing bowl. Using a hand-held mixer, mix for 2–3 minutes, until the mixture is smooth.

Add the cooled apple and fold through the cake batter. Pour the mixture into the prepared tin and crumble the streusel mixture over the top.

Bake in the oven for 50 minutes to 1 hour. It's harder to tell when cakes containing fruit are cooked through, but it should be golden brown, and coming away from the edges of the tin .

Take out of the oven and leave in the tin for 15 minutes, then remove and place on a stand or serving plate. Dust with icing sugar before slicing.

APPLE TARRAGON STREUSEL

SERVES 8-10

PREP 30 MINS,
PLUS COOLING

COOK 50 MINS

The title of this recipe is as much of a mouthful as the cake itself. It's like banana bread, but covered with peanut butter icing and homemade honeycomb. I could explain further but I think that says it all. It's not an awful mouthful to have, I suppose.

INGREDIENTS

For the honeycomb (makes 350g)
butter, for greasing
200g caster sugar
5 tbsp golden syrup (about 100g)
75g roasted peanuts, roughly chopped
2 tsp bicarbonate of soda

For the cake
100g unsalted butter, plus extra for greasing
175g soft brown sugar
2 medium eggs
2 ripe bananas, mashed (about 200g mashed banana)
225g self-raising flour, sifted
1 tsp baking powder

For the peanut butter icing
60g unsalted butter
60g smooth peanut butter
120g icing sugar, sifted
2 tbsp whole milk
100g peanut honeycomb (see above), crushed

METHOD Start with the honeycomb, which you need to make a few hours in advance. Lightly grease a large baking tray, preferably one with an edge, as once the magic happens, this stuff just travels. Line with baking paper.

Put the sugar and golden syrup into a medium pan on a medium heat and allow to cook gently. Have a cup of water handy with a pastry brush in it. Occasionally brush down the inner edge of the pan just above the sugar, to wash away any sugar crystals and help stop the mixture crystallizing. Once the sugar has melted, turn the heat up just a little and leave the mixture to bubble away, until the whole thing turns a rich amber colour (145–150°C on a sugar thermometer).

As soon as it reaches this stage, add the peanuts and stir through. Now add the bicarbonate of soda and stir it in really well. The mixture will bubble and rise up. Mix well and pour into the prepared tray. It will spread of its own accord. Set aside and let it cool completely. This can take a few hours.

Preheat the oven to 180°C/160°C fan/gas mark 4. Grease the base and sides of a 20cm round loose-bottomed cake tin. Line it with baking paper.

Cream the butter and sugar until light and fluffy.

Beat the eggs in a bowl and mix in the mashed banana. Add to the butter and sugar and mix to combine well. Add the flour and baking powder and fold in until you have a smooth cake batter. (As smooth as it can be with lumps of banana in it!) Pour the mixture into the tin and level the surface. Bake for 45–50 minutes.

Take the cake out of the oven and leave to cool in the tin for 15 minutes, then remove from the tin and leave to cool completely on a wire rack.

For the icing, mix the butter and peanut butter until combined into a smooth paste. Add the icing sugar and milk and whisk until light and fluffy.

Once the cake is completely cooled, smother it with the peanut butter icing. Take 100g of the honeycomb, crush it up roughly, and use it to decorate the top. In theory that should leave you some spare honeycomb to eat before you even get to the cake.

Peanut honeycomb banana cake

amber honeycomb, peanut butter icing,

banana sponge, let the magic happen

Every cake stand should have a simple Madeira sitting on it. When I go to a coffee shop, despite all the theatre that is a coffee shop these days, my eye always goes to the simplest thing on the counter. It's these cakes that are often the most special, especially if it's a small independent business, when that cake might even have been baked in someone's home oven, with all the love and none of the madness. In honour of simplicity, this is my Madeira with orange and almond.

SERVES 8

PREP 20 MINS

COOK 1 HOUR

INGREDIENTS

175g unsalted butter, softened, plus extra for greasing

175g caster sugar

3 medium eggs, lightly whisked

1 large orange, zest only (reserve the juice for the topping)

1 tsp almond extract

200g self-raising flour, sifted

50g ground almonds

For the crunchy topping
1 large orange, juice only

150g caster sugar

METHOD Preheat the oven to 170°C/150°C fan/gas mark 3. Lightly grease the base of a 900g loaf tin and line with baking paper.

For this cake I like to use an all-in-one method. So, whether you're using a stand mixer or a hand-held, put the butter, sugar, eggs, zest, almond extract, flour and ground almonds into the bowl. Mix gradually to start with, to avoid a cloud of flour in the air, then mix on a high speed until the mixture is thick, smooth and glossy.

Pour into the prepared tin and level off the surface. Bake in the oven on the middle shelf for 55 minutes to 1 hour. You will know the cake is ready when a skewer inserted comes out clean. The edges will have come away from the sides and there will be a slight peak in the cake.

Take the cake out of the oven but leave it in the tin.

Mix the juice of the orange with the sugar. While the cake is still warm, pour the mixture all over the cake and spread it out to create a crunchy citrussy topping.

Once the cake is cool, remove from the tin and enjoy in slices with a hot cup of tea.

ORANGE AND COFFEE POKE CAKE

This may sound like a suggestive social media expression, but really the name refers to the action of a spoon poking a cake. Nothing naughty here! (Unless you think cake is naughty, in which case this page is not for you.) This delicious moist coffee cake has holes deliberately poked in it after baking, and a thick tangy orange curd drizzled into them. I have as much fun making this as I do slicing it to reveal the hidden puddles of orange.

SERVES 9

PREP 30 MINS, PLUS COOLING

COOK 1 HOUR 15 MINS

INGREDIENTS

For the coffee cake

225g sunflower oil, plus extra for greasing

225g dark brown sugar

4 medium eggs

2 tbsp boiling water, mixed with 5 tsp instant coffee

225g self-raising flour, sifted

1 tsp baking powder

For the orange curd

6 medium egg yolks

3 oranges, zest and juice

100g caster sugar

25g unsalted butter

3 tbsp cornflour

METHOD Preheat the oven to 180°C /160°C fan/gas mark 4. Grease the base and sides of a 23cm square cake tin and line with baking paper.

Put the oil and sugar into a bowl and mix well. Add the eggs and whisk in well, then stir in the coffee mixture.

Add the flour and baking powder and mix until you have a smooth batter.

Pour the mixture into the prepared tin and bake for 50 minutes to 1 hour. The cake is ready when a skewer inserted comes out clean.

Take the cake out of the oven and leave it to cool in the tin. Then, using the handle of a wooden spoon, poke holes evenly across the cake. You need 36 holes – about 4 holes per portion – this sounds very exact but we want an equal measure of pokes per person. However, be sure not to poke the holes all the way down to the base of the cake, or the curd may seep out.

To make the curd, put the egg yolks, orange zest and juice, sugar, butter and cornflour into a pan and whisk it all together until combined. Pop on a low to medium heat, whisking all the time until the mixture thickens. It's ready when the curd coats the back of a spoon. Put the curd into a bowl and leave it to cool completely in the fridge.

Once the cake has cooled, take it out of the tin and put it on a serving dish or cake stand.

Put the cold curd into a piping bag and pipe it into the holes. When all the holes are filled, use the rest of the curd to cover the top of the cake.

ECCLES CAKE

SERVES 6

PREP 20 MINS

COOK 45 MINS

This is my recipe for an Eccles cake. Not Eccles cakes. Just one large, individual cake, to celebrate the wares of Lancashire, made with the same flaky pastry and fruity, citrussy filling. My family and I love to slice it when cooled, and eat it with hot custard poured over. I also like a slice simply as it is, with a cup of tea.

INGREDIENTS

1 x 500g puff pastry, ready-to-use, or frozen and defrosted

plain flour, for dusting

1 egg, beaten

2 tbsp demerara sugar

For the filling

15g unsalted butter

50g soft light brown sugar

25g mixed peel

100g currants

½ tsp ground cinnamon

½ tsp ground nutmeg

1 tsp coriander seeds, crushed

1 orange, zest only

to serve

hot custard

METHOD Dust a work surface with flour and knead the pastry for a few minutes. This is going against all the usual pastry rules. By doing this you are getting rid of the lamination and creating rougher layers. Wrap the pastry in clingfilm and leave it to chill in the fridge for 10 minutes.

Meanwhile preheat the oven to 180°C/160°C fan/gas mark 4. Line a baking tray with baking paper.

To make the filling, mix the butter with the sugar and add the mixed peel, currants, cinnamon, nutmeg, coriander seeds and orange zest. Make sure everything is well combined, then set to one side.

Dust the work surface with more flour. Take the pastry out of the fridge, remove the clingfilm, and roll it out to a circle about 30cm across. The pastry should be about 5mm thick. Put the filling in the centre and spread it out, making sure there is enough pastry left around the edge to cover all the filling.

Take the pastry from the edge and bring into the centre, pinching to seal as you go. Take a tray and slide the Eccles cake on to it. (This is where over-flouring will come in handy.) Put the prepared baking tray on top and flip it over so the pinched pastry is on the bottom. Dust off any excess flour. Now, using the palm of your hand, push the pastry down, just enough so you can see some of the fruit coming through. The whole thing should be about 24cm in diameter.

With a sharp knife, make 3 slits across the top, going all the way through to the fruit.

Glaze with the beaten egg, then sprinkle with the demerara sugar and bake for 40–45 minutes. After 30 minutes, cover with foil loosely for the final 15 minutes to stop the top browning too much.

You can eat this warm after 15 minutes or, like us, wait for it to cool. Slice it into wedges and eat with hot custard poured all over.

This is like a red velvet cake, but purple and with no artificial colouring. I am partial to a neon burst occasionally, but nature's food colouring is always the best kind, so this cake is tinted purple using blueberries. It's topped with an akutaq icing, which is based on a concoction of whipped fat and fruit made by Eskimos to satisfy their sweet tooth, using what little they have available. Inspired by the idea, I've come up with my own take on Eskimo icing, but with no seal blubber here! Best of all, this cake is entirely lactose-free.

SERVES 6-8

PREP 20 MINS

COOK 40 MINS

INGREDIENTS

For the cake

100g vegetable fat, plus extra for greasing

150g caster sugar

3 medium eggs, lightly beaten

1 tsp vanilla bean paste

50g frozen blueberries, defrosted and blitzed to a smooth paste

200g self-raising flour, sifted

1 tsp baking powder

For the Eskimo icing

100g vegetable fat

200g icing sugar, sifted

1 tsp vanilla bean paste

100g frozen blueberries, defrosted and drained

METHOD Preheat the oven to 180°C/160°C fan/gas mark 4. Grease the base of a 20cm round cake tin and line it with baking paper.

Put the fat and sugar into a bowl and whisk, using a hand-held mixer. Add the eggs, vanilla paste, blitzed blueberries, flour and baking powder and beat for 2 minutes, until you have a smooth shiny batter.

Pour the mixture into the prepared tin and level off the surface. Bake for 35–40 minutes, or until a skewer inserted comes out clean.

Remove from the oven and leave to cool in the tin for 20 minutes, then take the cake out of the tin and leave to cool completely on a wire rack.

Once the cake has cooled completely, make the icing. Put the fat and icing sugar into a bowl and whisk until the mixture is fluffy. Add the vanilla paste and the defrosted blueberries and mix really well, making sure you squash the blueberries to allow the juices to bleed out.

Spread the icing all over the top of the cake.

A simple baked cheesecake is one my favourite desserts. It can sit in the fridge and be enjoyed over the course of a week, and that ultimate slice is the best slice of all. But sometimes I feel short-changed by the base. It's nice enough, but often I want something more. So here I've baked a cheesecake without any base at all, and instead topped it with honey salted caramel and a chocolaty tiffin mixture. It's essentially a flipped-over version of the classic, but in my opinion all the best cakes are a little back to front!

SERVES 9

PREP 25 MINS,
PLUS COOLING
AND CHILLING

COOK 1 HOUR

INGREDIENTS

For the cheesecake
butter, for greasing

900g full-fat cream
cheese

200g caster sugar

150ml soured cream

3 tbsp plain flour

3 medium eggs, beaten

2 tsp vanilla bean paste

METHOD Preheat the oven to 160°C/140°C fan/gas mark 3. Grease the base of a 20cm round cake tin (it mustn't be loose-bottomed, imagine the leakage!), and line it with baking paper.

Put the cream cheese, sugar, soured cream, flour, eggs and vanilla paste into a large bowl and give it all a good mix, just for a minute or so, until it is well combined. You don't want to mix for too long and incorporate any air.

Pour the mixture into the prepared tin, tap it on the worktop to release any trapped air, then level the surface. Bake on the lower shelf of the oven for 1 hour.

As soon as the hour is up, open the oven door, leaving it slightly ajar. Pop a wooden spoon in the door to keep it just open and let out the heat slowly. Now turn the oven off.

Don't take the cheesecake out until the oven is completely cold. This recipe is more about patience than anything else. (Something I am generally not good at!)

Once the oven is cool, there's more waiting, I'm afraid. Put the cheesecake into the fridge to chill overnight.

→|

*For the honey
salted caramel*
50g butter

170g set honey

300ml double cream

½ tsp salt

For the tiffin crumble
150g digestives,
roughly crushed

75g unsalted butter

30g demerara sugar

50g dark chocolate
chips or chunks

50g toasted hazelnuts,
roughly chopped

Next day, it's time to make the honey salted caramel. Put the butter into a small pan on a medium heat. As soon as it has melted, add the honey and cook on a medium to high heat for 10 minutes, until the caramel is a golden brown. If it starts to catch, just turn the heat down slightly. After 10 minutes, pour in the cream, give it a mix and allow it to just come up to the boil. Take off the heat and stir in the salt. Set aside.

To make the tiffin crumble, put the biscuits into a zip-lock bag and crush them very roughly. I like a good mix of big pieces, small bits and lots of crumbs. Empty them into a bowl.

Melt the butter and pour it on to the biscuits. Leave to cool for about 10 minutes, while you take the cheesecake out of the fridge and turn it out on to a serving plate or platter.

Add the sugar, chocolate and hazelnuts to the buttery biscuit chunks.

Now for the back-to-front bit. Put the tiffin mixture on top of the cheesecake, but not in any neat fashion or packed tightly, just piled on top in peaks and troughs.

Reheat the caramel if it has cooled too much, and pour over the cheesecake.

For any of you who have had past cheesecakes fly across the table from the sheer brute force of fighting to cut a tight biscuit base, you are welcome!

STICKY PRUNE CAKE

Anyone who has children will know that prunes are a must in the house. They have magical powers that do special things to tummies from the inside out. Just one will usually do the trick, but my kids love them so much that they always try to sneak a massive handful. You can imagine the havoc that causes at 2 a.m. on a school night! But put them in cake and my goodness! This cake is naturally sticky from the soft prunes and is then saturated even more with a gooey toffee sauce.

SERVES 10-12

PREP 25 MINUTES

COOK 1 HOUR

INGREDIENTS

For the cake
200g stoned prunes

250ml boiling water

125g unsalted butter, plus extra for greasing

200g soft light brown sugar

2 tbsp golden syrup

3 medium eggs

250g self-raising flour, sifted

1 tsp baking powder

For the toffee sauce
25g unsalted butter

75g brown sugar

1 tbsp golden syrup

100ml double cream

a large pinch of salt

METHOD Preheat the oven to 180°C/160°C fan/gas mark 4. Grease the base and sides of a 20cm round loose-bottomed cake tin and line it with baking paper.

Put the prunes into a bowl and pour over the boiling water. Set aside and leave the prunes to rehydrate.

Put the butter and sugar into a bowl and beat until the mixture is light and fluffy. Add the golden syrup, then add the eggs one at a time, making sure to whisk after each addition.

Blitz the prunes and any remaining soaking water to a smooth thick paste. Whisk it into the cake mixture.

Now add the flour and baking powder and mix until smooth.

Pour the mixture into the prepared tin and bake for 50–55 minutes, until a skewer inserted comes out clean.

Take the cake out of the oven, but leave it in the tin.

To make the toffee sauce, put the butter, sugar and golden syrup into a small pan on a low heat until the sugar has melted. Stir in the cream, then leave to keep warm and thicken. This should take about 5–6 minutes altogether.

Pour the sauce all over the warm cake and leave it to soak in for at least an hour before you even think about serving.

In a lot of the sweet dishes I was taught to make while I was growing up, there was an element of toasting, be it flour, oats or vermicelli. I never really appreciated the flavour it imparted until I properly learnt to cook and bake. So for this simple take on a Victoria sponge I have toasted the butter and flour, and that's where all the flavour comes from. No spices. No extracts. Nothing else. It's a simple process that adds a subtle yet delicious new flavour to a classic recipe.

SERVES 9-12

PREP 20 MINS

COOK 35 MINS

INGREDIENTS

For the cake
200g unsalted butter, plus extra for greasing

200g self-raising flour, sifted

200g brown sugar

4 medium eggs

1 tsp baking powder

For the icing
150g unsalted butter, softened

300g icing sugar, sifted

1 tbsp whole milk

1 tsp icing sugar, for dusting

METHOD To start this cake we have to burn the butter first. Put it into a non-stick pan on a high heat until it is a dark amber brown colour. Take off the heat, put into a large mixing bowl and set aside.

Now it's time to toast the flour. Put it into a large non-stick frying pan on a medium heat and toast, making sure to stir all the time. This will take about 10 minutes. The flour will go from being white to brown very quickly, so keep a close eye.

Take off the heat and leave the flour to cool completely. When it is cold, sift the flour.

Preheat the oven to 190°C/170°C fan/gas mark 5. Grease the base of 2 20cm sandwich tins and line with baking paper.

Add the sugar, eggs, toasted flour and baking powder to the bowl of burnt butter and mix everything to a smooth batter. Divide the mixture between the prepared tins, then level the surfaces and bake for 20 minutes. You will know the cakes are ready when a skewer inserted comes out clean and the edges of the cakes are just coming away from the sides.

Leave the cakes in the tins for 15 minutes, then turn out on to wire racks to cool completely.

Once the cakes are cooled, make the buttercream icing by whisking the butter, icing sugar and milk till light and fluffy. Put the icing into a piping bag and pipe blobs all over the top of one cake. Sandwich with the other cake.

To finish, dust the top of the cake with a flourish of icing sugar.

I remember ordering peaches and cream at a café in New York. They served me some tinned peaches in a bowl with runny cream poured over them. Don't get me wrong, it wasn't horrible by any stretch of the imagination – after all, fruit with cream is one of the best combinations – but I was taken aback by how literal and underwhelming the interpretation was. It really was just peaches and cream. So I've decided to fix matters with my version, which is not quite so literal, since it takes peaches and cream, and adds cake. What's not to love?

SERVES 8

PREP 25 MINS

COOK 45 MINS

INGREDIENTS

For the peach topping
1 x 420g tin of peaches, drained

80g caster sugar

a few large sprigs of fresh lemon thyme

For the cake
100g unsalted butter, softened, plus extra for greasing

100g caster sugar

2 medium eggs

100g self-raising flour, sifted

½ tsp baking powder

For the cream
300ml thick double cream

1 tsp vanilla bean paste

2 tbsp runny honey

METHOD Let's start with the peaches. Once they are drained, put them into a bowl with the sugar. Mix gently, making sure not to break up the peaches.

Strip the leaves from the lemon thyme stalks. You need about 1 tablespoon's worth. Sprinkle them on to the peaches and mix to distribute. Be sure to reserve a few leaves for decoration later.

Preheat the oven to 180°C/160°C fan/gas mark 4. Grease the base of a 20cm round cake tin and line it with baking paper. It needs to be a fixed-base tin so the sugar syrup can't leak out.

Place the peaches in the tin, as neatly or unevenly as you like. Be sure to get all that lemon thyme in there too. Scoop out any leaves left in the bowl and dot them all over the peaches. Set the tin aside while you make the cake batter.

Put the butter and sugar into a mixing bowl and beat until the mixture is light and fluffy and almost white. Add the eggs one at a time, making sure they are well incorporated, then add the flour and baking powder and fold in until the mixture is a smooth cake batter.

Pour into the prepared tin, level the surface and bake for 40–45 minutes.

Meanwhile, make the cream part of the recipe by mixing the cream with the vanilla paste and honey.

Once the cake is baked, take it out of the oven and leave it to cool in the tin for 20 minutes. Turn it out carefully on to a serving dish or cake stand and scatter over the reserved thyme leaves. Your peaches and cream are ready – serve the cake in slices, with the cream alongside.

SERVES 10

PREP 30 MINS,
PLUS FREEZING

COOK 50 MINS

I grew up in a home where we didn't eat many desserts. So, the instant I discovered an ounce of freedom, it led me to a supermarket, where I would stare at all the cakes and always arrive home with bags full of everything except the items I'd been sent to buy. One memorable trip, I discovered an ice cream cake. It was so delicious I went back for another one the next day, only to find it had been discontinued! So this recipe is for all the poor discontinued cakes that could have been.

INGREDIENTS

For the cake

250g unsalted butter, softened, plus extra for greasing

250g caster sugar

5 medium eggs

250g self-raising flour, sifted

1 tsp baking powder

For the ice cream

300ml double cream

4 tbsp icing sugar

4 tbsp golden syrup

14g freeze-dried raspberries

100g cake scraps, crumbled (see method)

150g fresh raspberries

METHOD Start by making the cake. Preheat the oven to 180°C/160°C fan/ gas mark 4. Grease the base and sides of a 20cm round loose-bottomed cake tin and line it with baking paper.

Put the butter and sugar into a mixing bowl and beat until very light and fluffy. Crack in one egg at a time, making sure to beat well after each. Add the flour and baking powder and mix until you have a smooth batter.

Pour the mixture into the prepared tin, level off the surface and bake for 50 minutes on the middle shelf of the oven.

You will know the cake is ready when you insert a skewer and it comes out clean. Leave the cake to cool in the tin for at least 15 minutes, then remove and leave to cool further on a wire rack.

Once the cake has completely cooled, use a large serrated knife to level off the top if it has formed a dome. Pop any scraps of cake into a bowl.

Use a smaller knife to hollow out the inside of the cake. From the outside edge, come in about 2cm and cut vertically all the way round, creating an inner ring in the cake, but being very careful not to go all the way down.

Cut wedges in this inner circle as you would any cake, again making sure not to cut all the way to the bottom, then hollow out using a spoon. Put all the scraps into the bowl. You will only need 100g of scraps for the ice cream, so the rest of it can be a well-deserved snack.

Make the ice cream by putting the cream, icing sugar and golden syrup into a bowl and whipping to soft peaks. Add the dried raspberries and 100g of the cake scraps. Mix well. Put the mixture into the hollowed-out cake and level off the surface. Pop the cake on to a freezer tray and cover the top with the fresh fruit.

Freeze for a minimum of 2 hours. If freezing overnight, you may need to take the cake out of the freezer 15 minutes before serving so that it's soft enough to cut.

RASPBERRY ICE CREAM CAKE

SERVES 9-12

PREP **20 MIN,**
PLUS CHILLING

NO COOK

INGREDIENTS

For the base

250g digestive
biscuits, crushed

150g unsalted butter,
melted, plus extra
for greasing

For the cheesecake

600g full-fat
cream cheese

100g icing sugar

5–6 cardamom pods,
crushed, seeds removed
and crushed

1 x 300ml pot of
double cream

For the mango topping

1 x 420g tin of mango in
syrup, drained and
chopped into
small chunks

a handful of fresh mint,
roughly torn

This isn't an actual cake, but it is shaped like one and sliced like one, so it's nearly one, right? This is my go-to recipe whenever my mum visits. She likes simple, fresh desserts, and this no-bake cheesecake is perfect because it's so easy to make. The biscuit base is finished with a creamy cardamom cheesecake layer and a minty mango topping. Time to give your oven a day off!

METHOD Start by lightly greasing a 23cm round loose-bottomed cake tin and lining it with baking paper.

Crush the biscuits to fine crumbs and put them into a bowl with the melted butter. Mix to coat the crumbs, then pour them into the prepared tin and press them into the base, making sure to pack them all in tightly. Chill in the freezer while you make the filling.

Place the cream cheese in a bowl, sift in the icing sugar and add the crushed cardamom seeds. Whisk until well combined.

In another bowl, whip the cream to soft peaks. Add the whipped cream to the cream cheese mixture and fold in, using a spatula, until fully combined.

Take the biscuit base out of the freezer and pour or spoon the cream cheese mixture on top. Level the surface, then pop into the fridge for at least 1 hour.

When ready to serve, mix the chopped mango with the torn mint. Take the cake out of the fridge, transfer it from the tin on to a serving plate and top with the mango and mint mixture.

MANGO AND MINT
NO-BAKE CHEESECAKE

I am obsessed with bundt tins, which come in all sorts of interesting shapes and designs. The branded ones are not cheap to buy, but luckily lots of good bakeware shops have tapped into the craze and created their own, for which I am very grateful, as I don't want a cake tin to cost me a small fortune. For this recipe, the bundt tin gets a coating of icing sugar, which gives my light cake a sugary crust before it is topped with its zingy passion fruit glaze.

SERVES 12

PREP 30 MINS

COOK 45 MINS

INGREDIENTS
For the bundt
5 tbsp icing sugar
250g caster sugar
8 medium eggs
250g plain flour, sifted
20g unsalted butter, melted, plus extra for greasing

For the passion fruit glaze
pulp from 3 passion fruit
250g icing sugar, sifted
lemon juice

METHOD Preheat the oven to 180°C/160°C fan/gas mark 4. Grease the inside of a 2.8 litre bundt tin really well, making sure to get into every crevice. Put the icing sugar into the tin and swirl the tin around, covering it generously. Set aside.

To make the cake batter, put the caster sugar and eggs into a large mixing bowl. Whisk the mixture until it has tripled in size, which will take about 8–10 minutes. The mixture should be light and fluffy.

Add the flour to the mixture and fold it in, using a metal spoon, until it is incorporated. Be sure to be very gentle when folding in the flour, so that you don't knock out the air. There are no raising agents in this cake, and all the raising is done by the air you've just whisked into the sugar and eggs.

Mix until there are no more pockets of flour, then gently fold in the melted butter. Pour the cake batter carefully into the tin and bake in the oven for 40–45 minutes.

Once the cake is baked, leave it in the tin for 15 minutes, then turn it out on to a wire rack to cool completely.

Mix the passion fruit pulp and the icing sugar to a smooth glaze, loosening it with a little lemon juice if necessary.

Put the bundt on a serving plate and pour over the passion fruit glaze, spreading it over the cake.

SERVES 8

PREP 30 MINS

COOK 30 MINS

For this cake, I've taken inspiration from the queen of puddings, with its combination of breadcrumbs, custard, jam and a meringue topping. So this is the queen of cakes – and I don't mean Mary Berry, who is THE queen of cake – but her cake counterpart, its light sponge topped with jam and adorned with toasted meringue.

INGREDIENTS

For the cake
100g unsalted butter, room temperature, plus extra for greasing

100g caster sugar

1 tsp vanilla extract

2 medium eggs

100g self-raising flour, sifted

6 tbsp raspberry jam (about 160g)

For the meringue
2 egg whites

1 tsp cornflour

2 tbsp caster sugar

METHOD Preheat the oven to 190°C/170°C fan/ gas mark 5. Grease the base of a 20cm round loose-bottomed cake tin and line with baking paper.

In a mixing bowl beat the butter and sugar until they are light and fluffy and almost white. Add the vanilla, then add the eggs one at a time, beating well after each addition.

Add the flour and mix until you have a smooth batter. Spoon the mixture into the prepared tin and level off the surface.

Bake in the oven for 20 minutes, until a skewer inserted comes out clean. Leave in the tin for 10 minutes, then remove to a wire rack and leave to cool completely.

Put the cake on to a serving plate and cover the top with the jam.

To make the meringue, put the egg whites into a heatproof bowl that sits comfortably on top of a saucepan. Put a couple of centimetres of water in the base of the saucepan and bring to the boil on a high heat.

Turn the heat down and put the bowl of egg whites on top of the pan. Have a hand-held mixer ready and plugged in close by. Start whisking the egg whites and cornflour, then whisk in the sugar and keep whisking until it has dissolved. You will know this by testing it. Pick the meringue up and squeeze it between your fingers – if you cannot feel any grains of sugar, it is ready. If you can feel the grains, keep going until you cannot feel them between your fingers any more.

Take the bowl off the pan and keep whisking the meringue mixture until the bowl feels totally cool when touched on the outside. This can take 10 minutes.

Pop the meringue into a piping bag and pipe peaks all over the top of the cake. Now either toast the meringue with a blowtorch, or put the cake under a grill, making sure to keep an eye on it and rotating it if necessary.

By the time autumn arrives, we've usually eaten so much rhubarb over the summer that you'd think we would be fed up with it. My kids literally pick it out of the ground, wash it under the garden tap and dip it into their nan's sugar pot. I spent nearly a year living in the famous Rhubarb Triangle, so my love for the pink sweet stuff is singular. I love Yorkshire rhubarb like I love my Yorkshire babies! In this cake, the rhubarb stands tall (quite literally, as it's put into the tin vertically), and is combined with what, in my humble opinion, is its very best friend: ginger.

SERVES 8-12

PREP 20 MINS

COOK 1 HOUR
20 MINS

INGREDIENTS

150g unsalted butter, melted, plus extra for greasing

225g caster sugar

2 large eggs, beaten

1 tsp ground ginger

2 pieces of stem ginger in syrup, drained and grated

250g self-raising flour, sifted

1 tsp baking powder

3 tbsp whole milk

250g forced rhubarb, the pinker the better, cut into 8–9cm pieces (or at least as tall as your cake tin)

1 tbsp icing sugar, for dusting

METHOD Preheat the oven to 160°C/140°C fan/gas mark 3. Grease a 20cm round deep loose-bottomed cake tin and line it with baking paper.

Put the melted butter and sugar into a bowl and mix together. Add the eggs and whisk in until combined.

Mix in the ground ginger and grated stem ginger. Add the flour, baking powder and milk and whisk until the mixture is a smooth batter.

Pour the batter into the prepared tin and level off the surface.

Now take the pieces of rhubarb and poke them in upright. Try to space them out so there are even spaces between the sticks.

Pop the tin into the oven and bake for 1 hour 20 minutes. The cake should be golden brown, with spots of pink where the rhubarb has melted down.

Leave in the cake tin for 20 minutes, then transfer to a wire rack to cool completely. When totally cold, dust with icing sugar.

What's lovely about this cake is that if you use forced rhubarb, which is a vibrant pink, the white cake will have bright pink stripes that you only see when you cut into it.

Index

FAVOURITE RECIPES: ....

....

....

....

....

....

RECIPE IDEAS: ....

....

....

....

....

....

INGREDIENTS LISTS: ....

....

....

....

....

....

....

....

....

....

....

....

....

Someone told me at the very start of writing my first cookbook that writing cookbooks is easy. They lied. It's not! Writing a cookbook is one of the hardest things I have done and will ever do. But it's an experience I am so grateful for – every single time I write a recipe down.

Behind the scenes there are plenty of people to thank and who need to be acknowledged for all their hard work.

Thank you to Chris Terry for capturing pictures of the recipes (and me). I am proud of every single recipe from start to finish and you always make them look extra-special. Just when I think that's it, you show me another amazing shot.

Rob Allison and Rosie Mackean, I've never known people to rattle through recipes like you guys. Absolute machines. Thanks for all of your help banging out one recipe after another.

Emma Lahaye, thank you for making everything just as I would have it. You do wonders with some duct tape and little shifting. No place is sacred with you around, but for that I am grateful.

Huge thank you to the team at Michael Joseph: Ione, Sarah, Dan, John, Bea, Aimie, Yasmin, Amy, Louise, Claire, Laura, Jenny and Charlotte.

Massive thank you to Hungry Gap and the team who worked on putting the series together: Pete, Martha, Danny, Tim, Tom, Dave, Rob, Alan, Heather, Emma, Will, Natasha, Gayle, Jim, Lily, Kalpna, Sam, Joanna, Karen and Anne.

Thanks to Anne Kibel for joining the dots, crossing the 'T's and dotting the 'I's.

Thank you to all the people who, for me, are my home...

Mum and Dad – Asma and Jamir. Drive me insane as you do, it started with you. When all else feels frail, you are my home. Mum's curry in hand, Dad's hands on my head. That is where I feel safest.

Jasmin, Sadiya, Jakir, Yasmin and Shakir. I used to think it was daft that our names rhyme and that we all form part of a rhyming pair, a little bit like a dysfunctional comedy act, but I would not have it any other way. You are my right hand.

My nephews and nieces: Zayn, Aleesha, Deen Boy, Adhiy, Maya, Leela, Leeya, Idrees. Just when I think our hearts couldn't have any more room for another, another one comes along. Home needs an extension because of you guys, but we can work on that.

Abdal, Moses, David and Mary Moo. You are the people I take for granted the most, as we dart through life.

Abdal, did you make a coffee and not even ask whether I wanted a tea?

Moses, have you checked lost property for your trainers?

David, where's your packed lunch box?

Mary Moo, is that paint on the carpet?

We are so much more than the lost, the forgotten and the damaged. We are home.

MICHAEL JOSEPH

UK | USA | Canada | Ireland | Australia
India | New Zealand | South Africa

Michael Joseph is part of the Penguin Random House group
of companies whose addresses can be found
at global.penguinrandomhouse.com.

Penguin
Random House
UK

First published in Great Britain by Michael Joseph 2018
001

Set in Brandon Grotesque, Beton, Serendipity and Josefin Sans
Colour reproduction by Altaimage Ltd
Printed in Italy by Printer Trento Ltd srl

A CIP catalogue record for this book is available from the British Library

ISBN: 978–0–241–34899–4

www.greenpenguin.co.uk

MIX
Paper from
responsible sources
FSC® C018179

Penguin Random House is committed to a
sustainable future for our business, our readers
and our planet. This book is made from Forest
Stewardship Council® certified paper.